Hey Me, Where Have You Been?

An Introspective Path to Self-Awareness, Empowerment, and Your True Self

DEBORAH LIVERETT

Capucia LLC
211 Pauline Drive #513
York, PA 17402
www.capuciapublishing.com
Send questions to: support@capuciapublishing.com

Paperback ISBN: 978-1-954920-98-9
eBook ISBN: 979-8-9915156-0-3
Library of Congress Control Number: 2024919038

Cover Design: Ranilo Cabo
Layout: Ranilo Cabo
Editor and Proofreader: Heather Taylor
Book Midwife: Karen Everitt

Printed in the United States of America

Capucia LLC is proud to be a part of the Tree Neutral® program. Tree Neutral offsets the number of trees consumed in the production and printing of this book by taking proactive steps such as planting trees in direct proportion to the number of trees used to print books. To learn more about Tree Neutral, please visit treeneutral.com.

To RJ and JP (who rests in power-filled peace): each of your beings in this world have been the greatest gifts of my lifetime.

Contents

Author's Note

Iam sharing my soul in writing this book to shed light on the correlation between our thoughts and our feelings that they may be an opening to personal freedom to bring more kindness and love into our world. The Universe's energy has my (our) best interests at heart and the Creator of All is caring; these are two of my foundational concepts. Carrying these beliefs reminds me there is no reason to get upset about a change. I assume now that all change, even perceived initially as difficulty, is for my higher good because I cannot know everything that is about to happen. That is trust versus fear, trusting that everyone's good is paramount.

This is what I believe, and this is the way I find spiritual safety in a frantic world. I also have concluded that God is a lot smarter than I am! The Universal energy of God's creations is designed for harmony and peace. My fighting against that throws my energy off course. When I write about my relationship with God, I am not referring to my relationship with any one religious affiliation. I'm referring to God, the Creator of All Things—God, the Creator of Each One of Us. You may call It something else that is perfect for you. At times I may refer to It as Source, and others may think of it as Life with a capital L.

Whatever the term used, many of us believe in a Creative Source of some kind with many names. Humans created religion based on an interpretation of what were thought to be the attributes of God as presented in various verbal traditions and manuscripts. For me, God is the Creation Energy, and we are created by that Energy. Therefore, life is energy that resides in the body, the heart, and the mind as part of our spiritual being. Denial of the spirit energy is the missing piece of feeling in, and at, peace. Operating solely on the thinking-centered regulations of the outer voices, family expectations, government whimsy, mandated educationally and institutionally determined accreditations, media manipulation, and any individuals who *should* on you—without taking under consideration your desire to be your own self-directed, beautifully designed, blooming self—is self-sabotage. Our empowerment has been siphoned out of our memory. However, it remains ready for duty, and when asked, it can recover quickly because energy does not die. It can change forms, but it remains.

Introduction

The first hurdle to finding your authentic voice is accepting the fact that you have masterminded the life you are living, as have we all. At times, we do this unknowingly; our thoughts and beliefs are based on past events and cultural norms. The second hurdle is believing you deserve better for yourself. This is a sticking point for many of us. We believe: *If only people around me would change the way they behave, I could be happy.*

At some point you may have asked yourself: *Wouldn't life be easier if the people around me changed?* I call this the *if only* system of thinking. It's as if you instinctively know there is something else to have and another way to be, but you are stuck, not knowing how to change. The key is to open up to your true genius.

If you are saying to yourself: *I am not a genius*, take a breath. I am referring to your specialness, that assignment in your soul that you were sent to Earth with and to fulfill. If you have given this notion no thought, then you may have thought it doesn't exist in you. Perhaps you were deterred by naysayers while growing up.

I believe in Divine purpose and personal responsibilities. As this is part of my foundational belief, I deduce I have internal energetic resources to help me. The ideas, desires, and activities that come to you naturally for the good of yourself and the world are your genius. The things you do easily also house your genius.

My version of God, the Creator, gives us free will to do what we believe is necessary without judgment. What we believe is necessary may have nothing to do with God's idea for our creation. I trust we are here to learn how to shine our inherent light, and to create and share loving kindness with each other. Please understand, this is me. You have your own beliefs that support you, and I respect that.

If your beliefs allow you to spend the majority of your time consciously in the present moment, you can be creative within your life. You can curate new possibilities and new adventures. The goal is to live consciously, and staying conscious requires you to think for yourself. Some people find that difficult. I, however, have found it more difficult to live someone else's programming.

The commercial world doesn't want you to embrace your best self because when you do, it loses money. For instance, companies will lose money if you decide you don't need perfume because your natural odor is just fine, nor would you need makeup if you totally accepted your appearance. High-end clothing lines would be bankrupt, and dare we discuss the diet industry? How many hospitals and pharmaceutical companies would suffer financially if we were taking better care of ourselves?

I'm not saying there's anything wrong with any of the things listed above. I am saying if you need them to feel better about yourself, they are crutches. Feel really good about yourself and spray yourself with perfume if you want to. I certainly like a good perfume. Or if you're overweight, love your ample self, and be joyful as you pursue health. If you're too thin, love yourself as well, and be joyful as you pursue your health initiatives.

I am avoiding the trigger words that break us out into a cold sweat—the C word that triggers the ego to shut down our brain of all possibilities or any new thought: *Change*. As if change deters a precious life that isn't even the life you want, it's just the life you have accepted. Another C word is *Choice*. We believe choice is for other people while we try to remain faithful or loyal to what we committed to do or were told to do; whether it supports our knowing and growing ourselves has not seemed to matter.

This book is my attempt to encourage you to find the parts of yourself you have buried inside; those aspects of yourself that are built during conception and proceed to your birth to share with the world to make it a better place. It's important to believe in yourself. It's also important to hear when someone else believes in you.

I want you to know I believe in the truth of who you are and the gifts you bring to this incarnation. I have met thousands of people on my life journey and have been able to glean their inner light, their goodness—even when they say they can't find it for themselves. To all who are reading this, I share the following knowing:

I see your beauty just because you are here.
I embrace your strength-energy inside you when you think you feel tired.
I salute your Earthly mission and am delighted to encourage you to share
with the world what is in you.

Here's the offer I will make with you: Let us each open our minds and our hearts to this boomerang effect; you live in your loving genius that creates space for me to share my loving genius. If I see limits in myself and others, there is also a boomerang effect. Our energy swings back and forth. Conversely, I can live my genius and you have space to live yours rather than in our limited beliefs. Let's live in that space in which we can be our best selves.

This is not a book on manifestation as much as it is a plea to wake up to your extraordinary self to change your perspective beyond the self-imposed limitations that make you slug along rather than skip along in life. We all do it—thankfully not in all aspects of our lives. As we reimage how we live, we can open to the love, peace, and kindness that you and I deserve and desire—all while helping the needs of the world. We will spread Enlightened energy everywhere.

Trusting in an omnipotent energy to come through with what I need throughout the day releases me from worry, fear, and anxiety. One morning, I awoke from a dream that was so powerful, I immediately made the message smaller. I heard a voice in my dream say: *You are a mystic*. I woke up and immediately told myself: *No way, if anything close to that is true, I will label myself a mini-mystic*. A mystic is someone who takes time to observe all sides of situations. They can sense things and hear intuitive messages to help them and others in various situations.

The remainder of the week, I received supportive messages in emails, from television programs, and even from an astrologist who used my birth information to share this reaffirming message: *You are a mystic*. The synergy and synchronistic timing were undeniable.

I made my gifts smaller in my mind because I was comparing myself to a few of the great mystics I have read or listened to over the years. That awareness taught me not to compare myself to anyone else. Our light shines at the wattage we allow.

I had to wrap my thinking around that and do what I'm supposed to do, which is to share what I know to be true in a world that doesn't see the truth of differences as being wonderful, the truth of understanding that all our differences can make the world a better place. Those differences bring individual geniuses together to work collaboratively. We must leave the silos of *I am right* and detach from the notion that I and my tribe are the righteous and everyone else is not. We must prepare ourselves to step up, examine our thoughts and feelings to pinpoint where we are holding ourselves back, and question how we judge others who are different. Separation by similarities keeps us from new connections and continual growth.

There must be better tactics than stifling and killing each other. Self-hatred, cultural hatred, and cultural identity exclusively are not the answers going forward. Hatred is a tired and old paradigm that has not solved anything since the beginning of time. It may have felt like it worked for a few—perhaps the wealthiest, those with the most possessions. But that wealth does not mask humanity's gift to one another: compassion toward each other.

We are made of energy that draws us together simply because we are each human, connected by our mere existence and energetic life force that exists in each of us. We share our innate gifts and uniqueness with a vibration inside and between us all. Many of the wealthy who can afford any kind of experience still have their childhood insecurities, self-doubts, and unfulfilled sleepless nights, just like the rest of us.

Those thoughts prompted me to ask myself: *Is my calling to lift the veil from the mind's prison bars that keep my self-perception small, so that I can organize my walk and talk and let my inner light shine, the same way I ask people reading this book to do?*

With that thought, my ego said: *If you do that, then you're going to die.*

And my heart responded: *I'm going to die anyway, so I might as well die having done my greatest work here on Earth, which is to help other people. That is my calling. That is my purpose. I will carry no shame to my grave or into my next assignment.*

Then it was time for me to meditate because I felt excited, and I was scared, and both those feelings needed to be honored so that I could release to embrace what the Universe has in store for me. I must share my knowledge for the world to hear of another way of being.

You have no idea how scary and arrogant that sounded to me at first. But here is what I know to be true: Share who you are and the messages you came to Earth to share. Thank your highest self—your God-like figure, whatever you believe in that is all-good—thank them for giving you the courage and possibility of new and better growth and living.

We each have an ego that is part of our mind's perception. How we incorporate the ego into our daily life helps us to define our sense of ourselves. Our ego acts as an interpretive mediator between the soul (purpose, desires, instincts) and the outside world (societal norms, other people's opinions). The ego-voice believes it is our protector.

A healthy ego can create resilient thinking, by encouraging you to do something different when something didn't work out as planned. The healthy ego's approach is designed to build up your confidence. It can also remind you not to go down a difficult road again, if it hasn't served you well repeatedly. Ego can help you to be determined as you decide to face your challenges and how they have set you back, as well as open up to ideas of what you might do differently.

The ego has a two-sided function, one to motivate us to do and be more of what we came to accomplish in this lifetime. The other ego-side is fearful, judgmental, and puts up barriers under the guise of protecting us. I reference how this ego function sets up limitations throughout the book.

For instance, I am dismissing my ego-voice that is suggesting I stop writing. I do not have to manifest what my ego is suggesting. That ego-voice is a peace disruptor. I have power to stand in what I am given and allow deniers their position. That's growth and grown-up thinking on my part. My intention for today is to elevate my thinking of who I aim to be in this world going forward. It's a big intention that I am ready for because I read and listen for the Divine voice and elevate my understanding of unlimited potential. My desire in doing this is to shed light on a path for you, dear reader, to do the same, to grow and shine your brightest light. May the world need sunglasses when they are in your presence.

Chapter One

What If

What *if* questioning can be a powerful self-improvement tool. I use it to help me help my clients understand and clarify the relationship between the past and the present. For example, *what if* I had not had an ulcer at age fourteen?

But I did have an ulcer at that young age. Don't feel sorry for me. It was the best thing to happen to me because it introduced me to two concepts: *self-help* and *the power of positive thinking*. Serendipitously those concepts introduced me to two aspects I am grateful for these many years later: knowing the possibility of thinking thoughts that fuel new creation and the many books of now-deceased transformational author, Dr. Wayne Dyer.

Is Your Personal Past Affecting Your Present?

Dyer's books share exercises that helped me pay attention to what I was thinking throughout the day and taught me to shift my mind from that of an anxious teen to one of a calmer, more thoughtful young person. That awareness of the ability to change my perspective became my introduction to developing an aspirational goal of being an inspirational author to open people's minds to new and better-serving ideas for a more peaceful life. It stemmed from reading *Your Erroneous Zones*, practicing the exercises, watching Dr. Dyer interviewed on afternoon talk shows and, years later, watching him as a motivational speaker on PBS.

After the ulcer diagnosis, I began digesting ideas on how to grow mentally and behaviorally beyond my perceived circumstances. I overcame painful losses as a younger child, with my parents' separation, leaving my childhood home and moving to a one-bedroom apartment with one parent, losing contact with my father, and the death of my grandfather, who had been my loving, functional father figure. I had few coping skills in place to survive all that I had to endure, until I found motivational books.

Those formative years prepared me to spend the rest of my lifetime recognizing the importance of self-care and the need for mental and emotional congruence and physical and emotional compatibility. I gained an awareness of the beauty of synchronicity to enhance the importance of growing like a lotus, strong and mindful. Emerging from past murky situations and childhood hurts, I became mindful of trusting the inherent goodness in the world that we currently hear so little about.

What if my parents had not separated when I was seven years old? I may not have found my ability to intuitively feel others' pain well enough to assist people toward their own healing, as I have done as an adult. I sensed my mother's worry about the daily responsibility of rearing her child on her own, rarely having enough money to get by in the early years, and the stressing about the safety factors of raising a latch-key child while she had to work. And for me, there was the bonus of being an only child, which meant I learned how to entertain myself—another skill I still carry today.

What if we required ourselves to break from our habits of feeling disconnected to reaffirming ourselves despite our invisible emotional scars? We could create energetic spaces and decide to make a habit of feeling good inside. We could accept our right to be joyful and let that guide our thoughts. We could choose our emotions by choosing our thoughts consciously in conjunction with our subconscious mind.

What if it is time to release the habit of diligently berating ourselves? We all have the innate fortitude to think differently—to powerfully support brain, body, and emotions. We were born with this ability, and we can recapture it daily by examining our current beliefs and thoughts. Observe the destructive thoughts coming and going that you likely have been building since childhood.

Why write a book that touches on the brain and our emotions? I believe we can grow to our highest potential through the marriage of understanding and desiring change. The way out of the *what if* thinking is to discern which voices and ideas are yours.

As you tire of carrying the weight of thoughts that bring you down to your emotional knees, you can learn to cancel the thinking process that keeps you in downtrodden head and emotional spaces. Negative beliefs can hold you back from living an authentically fulfilling life. Declare as false the beliefs that do not support you and release them. Accept that you have carried each one long enough. Decide it is your time to use your personal authority to change. When you notice you are reverting to old, broken, and destructive thinking, stop yourself and say out loud, "I choose to restate that thought in a positive way because I deserve to feel good and to be better than I have been."

If that statement is too long, shorten it. Try instead: "I can choose differently again." You are coaching yourself into a positive frame of mind to improve your life and to be an example to those around you.

Ego, the Saboteur
By now, your ego-voice is probably getting louder. The ego's volume

is loud, and it is crass. It wants you to believe other people are better than you, and you have to prove something. It wants you to be cautious about yourself and everybody else. The ego sees its job as reminding you of what happened in the past while it creates fear, often regarding some future event or predicament. It holds on to negativity, and you become so entrenched in that way of thinking, you lose sight of the wonder you are. You believe the ego because you hear it so often in your head. You dismiss the good news that is trying to come through to you.

Here's the good news: You are in the present moment. You are not your past's keeper, nor are you obligated to drag it into your present moment.

Think about this: The ego-voice does not help you to feel good. The ego does not derive any pleasure from your understanding that you don't need its voice in your head. Begin to think of that harsh voice as the old foe you have kept around for so long, it drowns out your many accomplishments and prevents you from feeling your successes. The ego is the gaslight voice that silences all that is good about you.

The ego causes yearning in us all the time. Nothing is ever quite right in the ego-led mind. It is designed to keep us off-balance. As long as we are off-balance, the ego-voice in our heads can remain in control. It's cunning. It's manipulative, and it grows like a beast, towering over our dreams like the shadows of our childhood fears we saw on the wall. It seems so real.

Answer a few questions to help you determine how you want to proceed:

- Do you want to let go of the disbelief that you are bad or that you can't be celebrated?
- Do you want your ego-voice to continue to take all your attention, or do you want to experience peace in knowing your innate wonders?
- What do you need instead of the petulant ego?

You need to understand and accept you no longer want to be deceived. You can choose to silence the inner critic to gain some peace of mind. You want to admit when you've *been good* and when you need to make improvements for a more balanced life experience sans brutal and debilitating judgments. The heart desires us to embrace the understanding that we are all here to be celebrated in order to be free.

How do we get past and beyond what the ego is trying to tell us?

Believe it or not, it is by sitting still and listening to that small voice inside us who has been silenced for so long, we're not sure they're still there. I assure you they are there, dormant from neglect and alive in longing for a better and brighter life for you. The truth of who you are has been silenced, but it faithfully awaits your acceptance of your goodness. Its energy springs forth as you listen for and truly hear the kinder words that give you grace in the moment. It releases harsh judgment toward yourself and everyone else. Remember, what you pay attention to grows. When we accept our worthiness, we exchange higher energy within ourselves and with others.

Higher energy levels require higher levels of thinking. Get acquainted and live in concert with your best self. Make a list of your good qualities when you were living out of higher, supportive thinking spaces, so you can review the list when those sneaky and pesky lower thoughts reappear. If you can't think of any positive qualities about yourself, ask people you trust with positive attitudes what they see as your best qualities. Use the list to remind yourself of what is inside you and to grow steadily into who you were born to be.

Most of us can't see our energy with the naked eye; however, we can consciously feel when our energy levels are dropping below our ability to focus. We can feel the energy of hatred. It's cold and harsh with jagged edges tearing away at our inner being. We can feel the energy of Love—it's warm, accepting, and inviting. Joy is a natural and expansive energy; it wants to be shared with others. Everything in and around us is energy; that's a scientific fact.

One of the hardest lessons for me to grasp was that solid items, such as a wooden table or chair, have vibrational energy. When I opened my mind to a larger perspective, I understood that, while those pieces of furniture may appear hard and solid to the naked eye, they are made from trees, which are alive and therefore have energy. The table's energy is so dense we cannot see it with our eyes, but that doesn't mean there is not energy emanating from the wood. This helps us develop our awareness that we are energetic, spiritual beings having a human experience on Earth.

What if you allow yourself to be open to the energy of joy, love, and success on your terms? This is an important concept to grasp because it opens the way to see past misleading images and words that have been presented to us from childhood and carried into adulthood. If you are not having the natural experience of joy very often, you may be living under misleading images and thoughts.

Thoughts flip switches in the brain's neurological network. The brain and nerves analyze our state of being and produce internal chemicals to flow through our bloodstream in reaction to our thoughts. This is not a judgmental process. It is a spontaneous reaction initiated by the brain. We have the power to change that reaction by thinking more validating thoughts. This will lead to more positive feelings and chemical rewards in the brain.

The mind helps to control the biology in our bodies. For example, when you are newly in love with a person, the euphoria you feel is augmented by your brain, emitting the chemical *oxytocin* through your body. It creates a feeling of love and warm regard for this new person. When we are in love, a chemical called *vasopressin* is also released into the bloodstream to further promote our feelings. Love enhances the health of our internal systems, which are aided by these and other chemicals dancing through the bloodstream.

Conversely, as we encounter experiences that induce fear, chemicals in the form of stress hormones are released into the blood system to aid our immune system and facilitate reaction, such as fight or flight. Fearful thoughts can be generated throughout the day by watching television or social media responses on your computer or talking with friends about what you saw on the news or the disturbing thing your boss said. These can all signal the production of stress hormones.

The brain produces various chemical infusions to enhance these events as bursts of energy, such as clear eyesight to prepare you to take flight to safety when you sense danger. These chemical infusions can occur throughout the day and evening. Imagine the wear and tear on your body's immune system if you are in that cycle throughout the day. That fight-or-flight response is meant to be an occasional occurrence, not daily. However, it can occur more frequently than we desire, for example, while dealing with hostile interactions at work and dealing with disgruntled family or roommates at home.

Our thoughts, positive or negative, affect the health of our body. We choose: uplifting thinking to create greater health, or consistent, fear-based thinking to increase dis-ease in our bodies.

The reaction of fear hormones being released into the bloodstream should give us a screaming alert. *Danger!* Stop and assess what is happening around us. For years we were told we had inherited faulty genes from our family, and therefore we are likely to have the same diseases as our parents. While this may or may not be true, simply focusing our daily thinking on fear of the same disease can sometimes be the real creator of that illness.

Positivity may feel uncertain to you, and it may take some time to integrate it. New doorways can create new brain pathways that add to our understanding and awareness of how to achieve better experiences. If you aren't growing and are merely existing, staying in place, feeling hopeless, lost, or defeated, then you are not living your best possible life. We waste so much precious time.

We have this life, and perhaps we have an afterlife. On this side of life, aren't you tired of feeling bogged down, searching for relief outside yourself, believing it will be the magic elixir? The magic is in your heart and transmuted to your brain by your thoughts and beliefs.

Understand: your conscious mind encompasses your identity, your spiritual beliefs, your unique sense of self. It houses your creative desires and hopes. It governs the logical and rational aspects of how you view yourself. The more you stay in a present state of awareness, the larger the percentage of time you are in your conscious mind.

Your unconscious mind operates out of what is familiar; it stores like a computer everything you have heard and experienced since birth—and, some experts say, while you were in your mother's womb—to the current moments. From birth through seven years old, you are in observation mode, amazed at your environment, watching your caregivers' reactions, chronicling behaviors of the people around you, and believing this is the way of the entire world.

The unconscious may well hold our personal genius as well. The unconscious mind is so powerful, it works while we are sleeping. This is significant because if other people shaped our observations, we might not be living from what is important to us in our conscious and unconscious minds. Some researchers say that about 70 percent of what comes from the subconscious mind is negative and disempowers us from our true desires and meaning in life. The subconscious can construct limited beliefs that prevent us from our potential and possibilities.

Living from the subconscious means we aren't alert in choosing our life. We're simply going along as our stories are programmed in the brain's limbic area, which holds unpleasant and fearful moments from your past. Let's look at the example of harboring a victim mentality—a belief that speculates people are always trying to hurt or leave you. This is the message you tell yourself. It is a safety feature from the earliest years of humans to help them to remember where dangerous animals were lurking previously, so they could react to or avoid the scenario should it present itself again.

You may feel like a victim, but the powerful truth is victim mentality can become a conscious choice started in the unconscious mind. You are not obligated to take on those repetitive fears; however, it can be useful to notice how others manipulate you into replaying possible fears. Commercials for prescription drugs are frightening if you listen to them, and the news outlets use teasers to grab your subtle fear response that engages your brain to say: *I must stay tuned*, thereby hooking you into watching. Listen for the hook and watch where it leads you.

You can use the unconscious mind for positive good as well because, recall, it does not judge. Put the unconscious mind to work for you as you are going to sleep by directing your comments and questions to your subconscious mind. Ask it to focus on supplying answers to a problem you are having. Not only may answers appear when you least expect them, but you may also feel a need for shedding new light on how you can carry yourself in specific circumstances you want to change for the better. It may even appear in your sleeping dreams.

When you wake up, open your mind to new insights. The unconscious is a powerhouse when you partner it with a good night's sleep and your thoughtful questions. The unconscious mind is your inner resource that you may not have thought to engage with before.

I journal to awaken myself through my unconscious mind. My unconscious mind stores things about me and my past that I have buried and long since forgotten. Thoughts can bubble up while I write to help me understand myself and my reactions better. A shift opens my awareness, and I am able to see my motives more clearly. As I understand myself more, I can make changes more easily, usually recognizing that my perception of the past was a distorted view. My older and wiser self can see from new vantage points that not all things are as I had previously interpreted them.

The path to connecting with the conscious and unconscious is like a roadmap. Start at desire until you can articulate clearly what you are trying to do with this desire. Consistency lives in the hotel on your map. This is the sort of guidance and awareness you can ask of your subconscious before you go to sleep.

Wake up with an enthusiastic, open resolve to see things in new ways. Look and listen for synergies throughout the day. The roadmap points you to trust yourself. Be willing to stop and be still in nature or anywhere that you feel safe. Listen to the positive and wise messages that come into your mind.

Don't be so quick to dismiss any wise tidbit and slow the habitual talking points that have dominated a dismissal of loving thoughts in the past. Your harsh, negative, sad thoughts have had their time and have not produced anything new or helpful. Be willing to choose a different road on your map toward freedom.

Some people incorporate chanting, yoga, prayer, and meditation to help them. Don't be too quick to dismiss these methods just because they did not work the first few times you tried them. It took you years to develop the habitual thinking that has brought you where you are today. With greater emphasis and dedication, you can move to the brighter side of the map of your life. Open your mind to greater, more meaningful ways of living.

You get to decide—at what age or point in your life you will think for yourself? Mental maturity requires taking responsibility for your thoughts. Meaning: If your current way of being isn't creating the self-love, peace, self-acceptance, and joy that you desire, the onus is on you to change your way of thinking and thereby allow yourself to behave and feel differently. These actions go hand in hand.

When do you sit with yourself and ask clarifying, life-changing questions?

For example, if you hear yourself saying: *Well, I was taught not to be selfish*. It's a good principle to live by. However, if you find that you are often tired and anxious or pretending to be okay through self-neglect, then that principle has evolved into an excuse not to think about yourself or your needs. If you find that you are using sarcasm or insistent humor or even constant deflection to hold on to that principle, perhaps it is a good time to say to yourself: *Maybe that familial lesson is too extreme for me at this time*.

Consider it is time to stop blaming others for any dis-function you may have carried into adulthood. All caregivers from your childhood come with their own set of fears they unwittingly imposed onto young people. I suggest offering them grace; consider what they did was generally done to protect themselves as well as each tiny person in their care.

If you are miserable or not living to your full potential, then, clearly, you need to tweak those earlier lessons rather than dutifully kill your spirit to conform to a rule that robs you of your deserved and desired good. Only you can decide when you free yourself and pursue your own adventures. There are some people who inflict harm on children. To address this requires a set of skills that can be assisted by a good therapist. In my own life, I have come to understand it's likely someone hurt those people deeply, and they inflict that pain onto others. It does not solve their pain or yours. Your pain is your work, and your path to healing is possible.

Mind Shift: Connecting Heart and Mind

Journal, meditate, or ponder this:

Today I resolve to create a future different from my yesterdays. This requires taking on new ideas, changing perceptions, and letting go of mistakes—my own or others.

I embrace peace and joy now!

End your journaling or meditation with a similar statement in your own words.

Visualize opening a positive energy channel within yourself, envision its connection to your mind and your heart. Feel it pulsing to a calming rhythm; listen to the soothing beats of your heart and hear its uplifting message.

These true positive messages set you up to be your best self, the self you want to share to help us all be better. If it scares you a little, it could mean it's stretching you, but underneath it, there is a Peace of Mind because you know it's what your soul would have you be in order to be of service to yourself and others.

How can you say no?

You *can* say no, and probably have been for years and years. That nagging voice never stops. It's always lurking behind some corner to remind you there is more.

You will find different people also remind you there is more: more love, more peace, and a more positive outlook deep in the recesses of your soul that could be true for you. Your own small, internal whisper is urging that this is what you are here to do. It's a reminder of how you can be of help to yourself and others. That action could be in the smallest corner of your life or on the largest stage. It depends on you and your desire.

Now, if you hear nothing during your visualization practice, do not panic. You have pushed away your awareness of your soul's goals for so long, it may take time to allow yourself to liberate yourself from all the tamped down energy that you have been mired in.

Stay with the rhythm within you, and trust it is the coalescing union and alignment of your heart and your mind, and the messages will come. With practice, the messages will come more quickly; therefore, do not give up. You can trust the message is coming because the message already lies within you. (A list of all Mind Shifts and Exercises can be found on page 151.)

What if hardship teaches us to open our mind enough to change thoughts that disturb and agitate our body's operating symptoms, robbing us of our peace and squeezing out our ability to trust. The first time I had the above idea, my thoughts were a bulldog, growling at my heart with the intention of putting me back behind self-inflicted mental prison bars of fear and thereby negating love's abilities. For example, I would say to the Universe: *I believe he loves me.* But what kept me from allowing it into my heart? Did I want to be alone? Was I pushing away or not fully accepting it to avoid what I thought would be the inevitable hurt based on my past relationships?

Those thoughts created the belief that no one could love me. It took many days that led into months of self-reflection with numerous *what if* questions to deconstruct old messages as I understood the untrue premise. I had based my personal storytelling on someone else's created narrative that was handed down to me—some of which were lies revealed to me decades ago. Those misrepresented messages stayed with me much too long.

And why do people lie? There are many reasons. Here is a small sample:
- To take advantage of others or of a situation
- To cause pain intentionally and sometimes unintentionally
- To deflect punishment and to avoid being accountable
- To maintain the perceived status quo
- To create a scenario for others to think more highly of them, especially when their goodness isn't truly felt inside themselves

Be mindful of the thoughts that create a narrative you are causing based on your beliefs. Listen to your inner knowing when you hear information that does not add up. You may not have physical proof and, therefore, may choose not to react. Stay your desired course. When or if another truth shows up, you may choose to react in the way that supports your soul's goal to create an environment in which lying is not necessary.

Consider the Worldview

What if questions give us mental and emotional space to see perspectives and possibilities for ourselves as well as other people's points of view before we decide how to feel about an interaction. How our mind interprets what is happening in and around us determines how we feel about any incident or encounter, as well as offers us an opportunity to try something new or different.

Before a trip to Australia, I was challenging myself to say yes to new things, foods being one of them. Australia's dining delicacy is kangaroo, something not eaten in the United States. I shared with people that I would be trying kangaroo for the first time while in Sydney. The responses I received were varied but not particularly positive.

My understanding is if we grew up in Australia, it wouldn't seem strange nor out of place with the people in my communities. People around me did not see the broader perspective but were certainly curious upon my return—did I try it, and how did it taste? I found it to be delicious and felt pure joy that I hadn't let the opportunity pass me by based on a preconceived notion just because it is not offered in my home country.

What if there are other, higher self-awarenesses that are more Divine than we currently see or feel? If we can suspend what we think is happening and what we think we see just for a moment, we can master checking in for our most thoughtful reaction. To do so allows us energy and time to let more powerful, uplifting ideas shine through.

Don't fear; the world as you know it won't crumble in the seconds it takes to imagine safer, more peaceful interactions in our world, despite what you hear from the twenty-four-hour news cycle trying to convince you otherwise. If you are not living in a war-torn area, it is likely the news cycle is not reporting the truth of what is happening on your block. I live in Chicago, Illinois. People have asked me how I could live there because for years, the news coverage reported killings and theft at alarming rates. I can assure you that I have not run into the tragedies that are shown on the news. I am not saying they do not happen; the reports dismiss the good that happens, which is greater in number and safer than the devastation we see depicted on the television and various viewing platforms on social media.

Thoughts can obscure your worldview. We look at the surface story presented to us, make an immediate judgment, and prescribe a punishment as we see fit. We do not consider what people have been through, neither do we consider the causes and effects that created their behavior. The context is missing and likely one-sided, depending on the source of the communication. Apparently, others must be wrong for some of us to think ourselves superior, yet we are not, because each of us has our own set of gifts and shortcomings. We each take in the energy we give out. Be very careful how you judge lest you be judged internally. What we give out we often experience inside; we simply mask it and deflect it by pointing to others' shortcomings. Do not let the way you see the world obscure the loving conviction of the way the world really is, created in love to be loving.

What if you grasped the concept that whatever you focus on is what you see recurring in your life as it reflects interactions with others? You determine the energy you swirl in, no one else. We all go through what appear to be tough times, such as a family member's illness, unexpected job loss, another person's suffering or your own. This is when personal choice becomes your power. You can dwell in the hellish perception, or you can choose to accept and celebrate what once was and the good you find in a new situation. You can choose how long you will stay behind the mental bars that stymie you.

Sometimes you must be creative to find what there is to celebrate. When a family member is sick and caregiving is required, we mourn the loss of the person as they once were, accept the new reality, and meet the loved one where they are while remembering to take care of our own mental and physical self. I know some will say I'm making it sound easy. I have lived through some of these examples and a lot worse, and I know how difficult it can be without a strong mental attitude and a willingness to employ laughter to not take myself too seriously. Accept the uncertainty and ask for help to get through.

Someone loses their job unexpectedly; you say goodbye to that experience and say hello to what is next. Open yourself to experience feelings of expectant good coming your way. Why is this way of thinking so difficult to accept? Because we have been programmed to wallow in despair as the only appropriate option to a loss.

Toast good riddance to an ill-fitting job and focus on aligning your energy on the kind of workplace culture that will be a better fit for you, your skills, and your lifestyle. I know the worry about bills not being paid and not having enough money for putting food on the table. I grew up in a single-parent home where I was not allowed to learn how to cook because we didn't have enough money for me to create an inedible meal. Directly after my divorce, there were times I paid for groceries with a credit card because cash and payday were farther away than the immediate need.

These life infractions can find us focused too much of the time on what we don't want and not enough time on what we do want. This is critical because what we focus on is what we create. Look at your life, and if there is any area of despair, check your supporting thoughts of that despair. Do you see now how powerful you are? If you can create what you don't like by focusing on it; does it not stand to reason that if you turn your focus toward what you do want, your energy will lead you in self-perception, work situations, family, friendships, and romantic relationships? Most of us are doing well in one or two areas and just can't change the dynamic in others. You now have some insight as to how to get that off-track area back on the creation side and into more alignment with what you desire.

Mind Shift: Calling in Higher Guidance

There is an old adage: you cannot solve a problem at the level of thinking that you used when the problem was created. When I do not have any immediate solutions to conflicts or hurt feelings, I quiet my thinking to ask for Higher Guidance. Some people call it their Divine Energy Within Themselves. I recount the truth about where I am emotionally, how I am feeling, and what general outcome I would appreciate. Not anything specific; for example, I do not say: *The person must say they are wrong.* Rather, I seek a feeling solution, such as *to be at peace, that we may trust each other enough to discuss the situation.* Another favorite of mine is: *Please give me new insights.* The beauty of this hack is it can be done during the day while sitting or taking a walk or before falling asleep.

You may want to start with:

Help me, Inner Guidance, to clearer thinking!

I feel lost in an internal maze.

I feel the need to be very quiet and still to hear you more clearly.

Guide me, for I know not what steps to take.

I am grateful for Inner Guidance.

End your session with gratitude. This signals you to trust the answers are within yourself and will rise to the surface of your consciousness. Be willing to hear an answer, so you are more likely to notice what comes up for you. Pay attention and appreciate the smallest inkling you receive, that you may generate energy for accepting more insights. When you do it before sleeping, you are engaging your subconscious to work with you to help create what you need answered while you are asleep.

When you awake, lie still, and allow any new supportive thoughts space in your consciousness. Pay attention throughout the day. You may get an inkling in the shower or while driving or sitting alone. Do not dismiss new thoughts. Entertain the new thoughts. Try letting them loose in your mind or, if you are like me, on paper in a journal.

In relationships with others, I encourage people to talk about themselves and how they feel and what bothers them. I listen intently and ask clarifying questions, then probing questions, to get to know them better. I ask the questions to help them open and to try to expose their inner light to them.

Early on, I realized that toward the end of several relationships, I felt triggered and uncomfortable if the person was unhappy. Even if their unhappiness was not ascribed to me or something I said in the conversation, I would sit with my feelings after the conversation and notice my stomach would begin to churn. I would question whether it was me or our relationship that was bothering the person. I would look to my subconscious to reveal to me why I was so triggered and how could I stop it.

It took more time than I care to calculate when I first started to open myself up enough to hear the answer. It was a throwback response to monitoring my parents' relationship so carefully as a child. That was the source of my angst and fear in many of my closest relationships—separation.

I am thankful for reflection and an openness to listening to my inner guidance for healthier and more collaborative thoughts. I was so ready to heal this misbelief that I had carried for what felt like centuries. This was a gratitude moment in my growth—gratitude for feeling love and for awareness that shone a light on what was happening and how I could change my thinking for my own peace of mind.

Let your awareness be a thanksgiving reminder to you when you are in dis-ease with what surrounds you inside and outside yourself. Take notice of how you feel and how you are going about this life, feeling its harshness. Allow yourself to sit with it and allow your answers to be originally focused. Feel in the present moment the answers are a relief. If you aren't comfortable initially, understand sitting with your discomfort for self-evaluation can feel unfamiliar.

Set a timer for sixty seconds, five minutes, or longer if the tactic does not seem daunting or too consumptive of your time—a precious resource. Stop at the appointed time, and ask your authentic inner guide: *What lesson you would have me learn?*

When more of what creates angst shows up, don't do what we often do: We declare to ourselves nothing works, or we say: *I always feel this way because my life sucks.* Remember our task is to change the thought process. Remind yourself first: *Oh, this is happening again to teach me something about myself or my life choices.*

Then try asking questions such as these:
- *What about this makes me feel so out of control?*
- *Why do I feel insecure?*
- *How can I change?*
- *What resources do I have to help me create different ways of thinking?*
- *How can my reaction change in situations like this?*

Your first and ultimate internal decisions are:
- Do I want to feel better?
- Am I willing to think differently in order to become my best and more peaceful self?

If you are tired enough of your current situation, the answer will be yes to both. When you voice your yes, there is a chance a harsh critical voice—your ego—will arise or churn in your heart or stomach; just remind yourself that old thinking is no longer your truth.

Change Your Self-Talk

You have declared that you are ready to think differently to feel your best self. The same kindness you show others, you can show to yourself. The kindness you show to others means that kindness lives in you, and therefore you are fully capable to turn kindness toward yourself. You have the power to change when you realize that you have the power. You have the power of an unbreakable creation you were born with that we call *Love Energy*. That energy resides inside you always.

Change what you say to yourself. For example, if you think of yourself as a not-exceptionally smart person, change your personal narrative to: *I am smart*, and each time something smart comes out of your mouth, take a moment to smile. Acknowledgment builds new awareness so acceptance can follow. If you don't believe you are smart in whatever instance you're in, but someone says thank you for what you said or contributed, make no excuse, and again smile at yourself in agreement.

If you are in a group setting and want to say a particular thing, but someone else says it first, that's a good time to remind yourself you have smart thoughts. Reinforce to yourself you are smart when everyone else is seeing it but you. Repetition is key to effecting change and building confidence. Remind yourself regularly that you are smart. Linger in acknowledgment for more than thirty seconds. It helps the brain create pathways to acknowledge what you think about yourself.

Forgive the people who planted the seed of doubt about your intelligence because they knew not what they were destroying. They did not understand that your self-worth and your self-image were tied to what they were saying. Understand they were acting out of their past experiences, out of what they may have been taught. Perhaps they dealt with cruelty that developed into their own sense of insecurity in their lives.

You can embrace the knowledge that what they put on you and in your head no longer needs to be your truth. How you lived as a young person was the best you knew at that time. Don't give credit to their feedback any longer if it diminishes your understanding of yourself. Others cannot define you unless you allow it. Advance your thinking about your identity based on who you want to be and how you want to present yourself to the world. No one had the perfect crystal ball to predict who you would become, without your permission. You have a right and responsibility to change your thoughts about yourself for the better.

The reason I suggest those thoughts need to change is we were not designed to feel bad about ourselves. We were designed to love ourselves and love others. Change your behavior, which changes the way you react to yourself. You don't feel bad because you are a bad person, you feel bad because you think you're bad. You feel inept because you don't think highly of yourself or any of your achievements. The feelings of ineptitude and badness are in direct opposition to the truth of who you are, and that is causing the breakdown from within yourself. Your being alive and in this world makes you worthy of being thought of in the most loving ways.

Have you ever wondered why is it okay to say hateful things to ourselves about ourselves?

Would we waiver, as in reject, if we heard someone else say it about themselves or anyone else out loud?

Likely yes—if we know the person. Substitute yourself for that person. That becomes reason enough to get to know your authentic self and not the personality mask you currently show the world.

What are your recurring tendencies in work, romance, family, and community relationships? This is where your observation continues, when your critical voice says: *This will make me happy*, and then you notice the situation or person doesn't behave a certain way. Now your ego—the same as the critical inner voice—is telling you *they* are out to get you, and that becomes your overriding thought. This is an example of a recurring theme of mistrust in others. Our ego-voice cries into our broken heart because the person in the situation is not behaving as we thought they would.

Your first response to this way of thinking about others is to ask yourself:

- *What is my lesson to learn?*
- *What is the most loving thing I can say for me and this person?*

- *What is the most loving thing I can do in this situation for this person and for myself?*

Identify your natural tendency for coping in recurring life situations. Some like to argue, while some blame and shame the other person. My tendency was to say: *The heck with this!* And leave. I finally noticed the pattern and became grateful for the wakeup call to shake the long-held belief that I was not safe and needed to leave before someone could hurt me.

I worked to break down this core belief I had been carrying and recreating. I had to get tired of crying before I could shift the pattern. I had to be tired of not trusting situations and myself. I wanted to understand what the Universe wanted me to take away from those recurring situations. I had to concede the ego-voice in my head wanted me to think its voice was right, and it was simply trying to protect me.

Yet in order to grow emotionally and mentally, I had to trust I would be the best-qualified person to determine my direction in various situations. My inner guidance would say: *Don't speak yet.* So, I didn't speak. I waited for internal guidance to speak through me, and I did not allow my bruised ego to speak for me. In the beginning of my transformation walk, I would wonder what part insecurity played and what was my emotional state.

If I trust in a higher power that wants my highest good, I can be still. I can exert personal agency to not react in the moment. I can promise myself after thinking it through I can revisit what happened with the person.

Taking Personal Responsibility for Behavior

Personal responsibly is a master key to change. It is an inner responsibility. It is not: *If only someone else would change, I could be happy.* It is not: *If only I lived somewhere else, I could be at peace.* Peace is a personal choice unrelated to anything outside yourself. Inner peace exists when you can align your thoughts and your emotions and decide to be peaceful. To place the responsibility on others is to ensure that you will not have inner peace.

Waiting for someone else to dictate how you feel about yourself is akin to being a human yo-yo: up and down emotionally, depending on someone else's behavior, words, or sacrifices. Searching outside ourselves for answers depends entirely too much on the whims of others, who are pretending they know what's best for us. Sometimes they are so closed-off emotionally, they don't know what's best for themselves. They get by in their pretend, coverup mode.

Let's look at this ordinary situation. You are in your car, and someone cuts you off in traffic. Your reaction is commensurate with your perception of their behavior. You have likely labeled them a *bad driver*. You get upset. When you get to your destination, you tell everyone who will listen how rude this person on the highway was to cut you off. You settle into your chair and find it difficult to concentrate. You think maybe a cup of coffee will help.

How much time has passed since the incident? An hour, maybe two. The offending driver is getting on with their day after the three-second incident, and you are still holding on to it. Who is being harmed, and who is responsible for how you feel and have felt in the last hour or more minutes of precious life?

As long as you can blame someone else for your anger, you remain powerless. It's an excuse to stay put and emotionally stuck. When you take responsibility for your behavior, you can initiate change. You open the door to understanding what is lacking or hurting in you. Your anger is not about the other person. It's about you and whatever you are hiding or covering up.

How would you want someone to treat you if you made a wrong movement? The way you are reacting, or in a different way?

Standing in your own desires is not a call to create misfortune for others. It's not a sanction to rob anyone of their own growth potential. It does not call for you to be cruel to another person or to mislead them for your own gain. That creates more hostility in the world, and we have enough of that. Sharing your self-awareness and innate gifts creates space for others to share theirs. Giving grace to ourselves opens space for another to receive grace from us. The energy of brotherhood, sisterhood, and community working for mental and spiritual well-being benefits us all. As we grow in this way, we have an obligation to understand more deeply our emotions and our journey.

I have found that a positive *foundational belief system* is very helpful in making changes for a better life journey with myself and the communities with which I am engaged. These beliefs are my go-tos when things are going awry. Reviewing them and repeating them in my mind help me to find my balance rather than being swallowed up in an abyss of sadness.

I discuss how to create your own foundational belief system in Chapter Three.

Chapter Two

Emotional Beings

Emotions are our mental reactions to what is happening around us. There is an understanding that *emotions* and *feelings* are related. I find the terms are often used interchangeably. Some say emotions are internal sensations that we label as various feelings. Other authorities characterize emotions as internal energy's motion ignited by our mind's thought system.

Emotions are aligned in the brain. Our *amygdala* stores pleasant emotions we can learn from, fearful emotions from threatening situations, and memories of our reactions to events at that time. Those memories then influence the *neocortex*, which relates to our emotional processing, switching on an alert when there is a threat or stress within our current environment. The neocortex is responsible for our feeling sensations—sensory input, such as taste, touch, smell—our cognition, and our consciousness. The *prefrontal cortex* tries to assist the amygdala by making the stressful events seem a little less frustrating, which can successfully slow the production of *cortisol*—a hormone released during times of stress. When the amygdala is activated, we feel our emotions more intensely, usually as aggression or all-out, paralyzing fear.

Emotions can be a reaction to outside influences, such as seeing a happy, laughing baby or hugging a good friend who is crying or remembering a special moment. These influences trigger biochemical reactions. Simply thinking of the circumstance that created an emotion can stimulate that same biochemical reaction. Your brain stores thoughts, feelings, beliefs, imagination, and attitudes. Your mind is unique, built from past experiences and interactions as well as what you, as an adult, tell yourself. This is one reason family members remember different versions of the same event—because our thoughts create our own dialogue and memory. Memories are stored in the subconscious mind, and they create perceptions unique to you as the thinker.

We feel unhappy when we cannot sit in the world's view of what others think we should be, think, and do. That is part of a mistaken belief system: When we try to conform, we are going against what is right for us. Your job is to be your authentic self, in tune with your innate understanding. When we act outside our innate intelligence, we create discord within ourselves.

The world would have you believe that you should feel discounted within because you're not doing, being, or saying what they deem you should be. But the only sources who know your true being are yourself and the Highest Creator of you. Not your parents, grandparents, traditions, nor any human guardians.

Personal Awareness

We have a smaller self and a Taller Self. As an adult, your smaller self is the hurt representative—your child-like self—who resides inside you. Likely they have not received the nurturing they need to allow you to return to your authentic, Taller Self. I'm not referring to your body height. I'm talking about our inner being. The small self represents the harsh self-critic, a frightened, hidden, shy little self, too scared to be seen while longing to be heard. Your authentic Taller Self is the healed representative known as your emotionally and mentally mature self.

In my corporate career, I led coaching sessions with various groups. In one session with a group of women, we were defining what it meant to be one's authentic self in the work environment. As they spoke, I felt uneasy because I could sense that, while they believed what they were saying, my empathic abilities felt from their nervous laughs and their false bravado that they were not speaking the truth of their beings.

It took me a while to figure out why I was uneasy about the direction of the conversation, until I realized they each spoke from their wounded perspectives, and at times I had likely responded the same way.

They said things like: *I don't take anything from my coworkers or bosses. I set them straight when they talked to me in a way that I didn't like.* Some let their anger unleash, and that took the lead in most of their interactions. That felt authentic to them. We got to the end of the session, and I had to quickly wrap up. But the session haunted me to a small degree because it's the perception and viewpoint of so many people who are marginalized and whose mental concept was solidified in their unexamined childhood upbringing. They bring the hurt of how their childhood origin shaped them to think and feel to face the outside world that may or may not be coming for them.

Emotional maturity is birthed when you decide to manage your emotions, which includes feeling and acknowledging your emotions, exerting control over your rash impulses, developing your abilities to adapt and be flexible in situations, and connecting and understanding your self-awareness to help manage your various interactions. Through these reflections, you bring the ability to have a higher self-regard and growth in your optimism with the people and circumstances around you.

In your interactions with others or when watching disturbing information, recognize when you think and feel upset. By taking a moment to understand why you are upset or triggered, you can take time to decide how you wish to be recognized. When we, not those around us, manage our emotional selves, we see the world around us change. Those changes activate our curiosity and prompt us to ask nonjudgmental questions of ourselves and, when we are calm, of others. Seek understanding and options in your thinking.

Understanding another's backstory takes the personal sting out of the interaction equation, which then opens space for alternative thinking. You can move away from labeling someone as wrong or bad. Rather, you can look at alternatives and options for their behavior. With various options, you can meet them in the middle and create space to share what matters to each other. Together, you can create a solution. This examination starts with questions to help you understand yourself better.

Sample starter check-in questions with yourself:
- *Why am I resisting what is happening?*
- *What happens if I choose to continue resisting what happens around me?*
- *What are possible options to think through this situation?*
- *Which option can I use to choose consciously?*

There are numerous options for any situation when we are clear on the emotions and thoughts that capture our focus. As we examine those options, start with agape and fear, the two primary emotions.

Agape is the purest form of love, the living light born in us from Universal Energy. *Love* is the ultimate expression of our soul. *Love* is the authentic self that shines in the form of joy, acceptance, nonjudgment, happiness, excitement, connectedness, and gratefulness. It is the power to be oneself and to share that self for no reason other than to be *Loving*. We can further define authenticity as our innate intelligence or our inner genius, which is the wisdom that lives inside each of us. It is as individual as each and every one of us. It is living your inside truth outwardly.

Fear is an essential human emotion that has become pervasive in too many of our present-day settings. It was programmed in our nervous system to alert us of immediate physical danger, compelling us to notice what is happening and to flee from that danger or to fight. However, in today's world, people are walking emotionally wounded, carrying fear around every corner, causing an avalanche of other emotions that consistently secrete chemicals from the adrenal glands.

We walk around with feelings of impending panic, anxiety, doom, or dread. Warning signs are represented by a multitude of emotions and feelings. We experience bitterness, confusion, depression, devastation, disappointment, distrust, frustration, grief, guilt, hate, hurt, judgment, loneliness, melancholy, overwhelm, powerlessness, pridefulness, resentment, sadness, shame, stress, worry, and so on. Fears can be present in the halls of your workplace, home, means of transportation, or while you're walking out and about in the streets. Letting fears take over your mind-space continually can stymie creativity and rob you of vitality and the influx of new possibilities.

Other emotions can be considered a subset of either agape or fear. The subsets do not need to be judged as good or bad so much as they are alerts to help you decide what you need to do, think, be, or believe to achieve your positive purpose. As an added bonus, I have included an Emotional Digest that lists subset emotions and feelings at the back of the book. There may be times when you feel something but cannot figure out what it is. The digest may give you some insight to what you are experiencing in the moment.

As children, we forget how to love ourselves, seeking approval from the adults we believed to be our, shall I say, God-like figures. Moving away from loving acceptance of the self, we take on a pile of fears that cover up self-love. However, as we grow, if we can believe in something that is greater than what we see in the world, we can call it what feels right for us. God, Energetic Beauty, Our Ultimate Source,

Allah, Jehovah, Buddha, and Mother Goddess are a few of the names. Call that Source whatever works for you and your heart.

Your heart space and soul's goal are in direct energetic contact. Your loving self aligned with your soul's goals are the agreement you made prior to taking on this realm of being. Love light is your original state of being, not the accumulation of the protective shell you hide behind to survive in this world. I am not referring to the house you lived in as your original state of being. Your birth state of pure Love started your authentic self-journey. As an adult, your loving self can show up to do the work of your soul—perhaps it feels like it must.

I choose to see all feelings as a gift. Even those that don't feel great can be a blessing. Emotions are our inner intelligence. They can lead us with their whispers of truths that we can't hear from others. Emotions are our closest assets when heard from the heart and mind connection. If our emotions are coming from our wounded thinking, likely from the past, it can distort our connection to what is being heard in the present moment.

Our thoughts travel through time and space, while the body is right here in the present moment. Our body's condition is partially created by our thoughts and emotions, which impact the body's physiology. Often stressful problems become more problematic based on the severity and frequency of the stressful or traumatic stories we tell ourselves, not necessarily what is happening in the present.

Mind Shift: Be Present

Perhaps you wake in the morning and realize your mind is running a marathon, causing you a frantic panic wave of all you have to accomplish in this day, and then thoughts of yesterday's hardest moments begin to swirl. Anxiety makes jumping out of bed seem like an Olympic sport you haven't trained for. You need a system to return yourself to the present moment, because none of the scenarios roaming in your head are actually happening. We can re-train ourselves to wake up and be present and silent rather than allowing our minds to revisit the past or turning on social media or the television.

A breathing exercise can quiet your thoughts and return you to the present moment at any time. Your energy changes and can deliver you from the loop thinking that does not support your highest wisdom and uplifted feelings.

As you wake up in the morning before your first thoughts take hold, inhale deeply and claim in your mind:

I am calm.

Release your breath slowly. Repeat as many times as you can to move with no hint of old thoughts of the past, nor any hint of heavy expectation for the day to come. When you get in the shower, continue to focus on breathing, the water, and the soap. If thoughts of the day begin to creep in, give them no judgment, merely return to your breathing deeply in and slowly out.

When you are out and about during the day, you can do this, and no one will be the wiser. Breathe in and breathe out. Focus the breath on your claim for calmness with each inhale and exhale.

Now is all we have in every moment. Delving into reliving and holding on to the past or projecting into the future creates havoc on our mental health and vibrational energy, all of which can hinder your authentic self from being present.

You must lay down the notion of comparison and one-upmanship to claim your unique self and honor your gifts and mission on Earth. We accepted a charge when we came here to share those very gifts. Sharing one's gifts freely requires loving and accepting ourselves and others.

There is a desire and a need to do what you came here to do, to express what you came here to express. And I'm not talking about a reality TV kind of appearance, hiding yourself behind antics and upset. Rather, you have a gift that can be shared right from where you are—your work, your mission—that gives space for others to work their missions. There is no need to compare or compete because you're doing what you know in your core is yours to do or say.

There is room for each of us to share our gifts. To share our gifts, we need knowledge of our emotions. Emotions can range and cross over between fear and love. Anger as a beginning catalyst for change should be explored. For example: anger toward a perceived unjust situation can propel us into movement to create change. That anger is powerful at the beginning of any change movement, but it's not enough to sustain a movement because that energy is on a lower vibration, depletes us quickly, and is difficult to sustain.

While anger can fuel you in the beginning, you need a developed strategy and like-minded people to help you move forward and to assist you to think in new ways. If people can get hurt with your words or physical force, don't do it because that can set off another round of lower-energy results.

An example of anger crossing over to love can be when it is used as a cry for setting boundaries and fulfills a need to help propel you into harmony within. We do not dismiss our emotions and feelings.

We view them for the lessons we need to learn about ourselves. Think of anger as a wakeup call to do something different. Anger is a lower vibration and can waken quickly. When the lower vibration wanes, you need a different and higher vibration to continue strategizing to your highest desire or calling. Use anger to help you start and allow a higher vibration to propel you toward your highest desire or call.

I recall a friend of mine having an argument with an ex-spouse. My friend got into her car and angrily drove away from the house they once shared. Two blocks from the house, she accidentally rear-ended a car in front of her. She was crying even though no one was hurt other than the cars. She could not see at first what was miraculous about this incident that we call an accident. She finally realized driving while angry is not a recipe she would follow again.

Emotions can affect how we react. Angry emotions can affect our reaction time. Low-level emotions can blur our perceptions of what we hear and can obscure our judgment. Notice I didn't say at any point that emotions are *bad*. Our emotions can blur perception in a positive way or in a negative way. A few emotions and feelings can border between both *love* and fear: vulnerability, anger, and disgust.

Goodbye Oppression

Cultural oppression inflicts biased perceptions that devalue other cultures, ethnicities, genders, abilities, ages, personalities, and orientations with a set of fabricated interpretations and filters. Prolonged unjust control and harmful treatment can prevent people from expressing their emotions, talents, and genius.

When we are taught that it is neither safe nor appropriate to notice and express feelings, our inner development is clipped. When we were told to stop crying, "before I give you something to cry about," we stopped crying and disconnected from our denied expression. Expressing feelings becomes unsafe in that type of environment.

Disconnecting from feelings and emotions can cause anxiety within us. That disconnection can be so imbedded for so long, we can't recall why or how it began. We can't point with certainty to why we are feeling this way. Children will grow into adults who distract themselves from feeling. The behavior may be linked to avoiding embarrassment or shutting down the energy of exposure to others.

Those who don't give in to others' need for dominance can see and sense there is nothing wrong with who they are. They live in a way that says: *I can show you better than I will tell you*, which they can do because they see beyond what is being said to embrace their own life. This awareness and stance may not be automatic. Some take a long time before they decide to no longer listen to or believe others. They can take charge of their own destiny when they let go of others' dominance.

A person's need to dominate another is a loud scream there is something lacking within that person's sense of self-worth. If you have to oppress someone to feel good about yourself, you don't inherently feel good about yourself, and you won't feel better by putting someone else down. The oppressor may feel inadequate and fearful—so much so, they use words, laws, and deeds to subvert other people's inalienable rights. No one has the authority to usurp your right to be who and how you came here to be.

When people refuse to take responsibility for their feelings, they may say things like: *He made me feel so angry*. Here's the deal: No one can *make* you feel anything. Your mind creates a story or scenario in which you believe the other person pushed your buttons, causing your anger.

Where our mind goes; our reality seems to grow.

There was a time when men were thought to be less manly if they were crying in public. People called it a sign of weakness. Tears communicate a deep and meaningful message to others. The act of crying and the responses elicited by those tears confirm we are connected. Tears indicate emotions of happiness, sadness, or even overwhelm. We were told when we were growing up that crying—something fundamental to the human spirit—shouldn't be exhibited in public, but we know intrinsically shedding tears recognizes we are not alone.

The benefit of emotional crying when triggered is that the brain releases endorphins that can release pain and improve our mood. Our tears can signal to others we are in distress or feeling sadness, and this can increase our connection to others. Tears can evoke the idea that we need help from another, creating an attachment. When we can trust another person with our tears, their comfort can feel like a welcome pacifier in our time of need.

When parents tell little boys: *Crying is acting like a girl*, we are telling them to suppress their emotions and to think less of girls for their display of emotions. When parents tell girls: *Stop crying. You have nothing to cry about!* they are shutting off the girls' authentic awareness. How can we expect our children to grow into caring people without awareness of emotional release?

When we prolong our silence about what is happening within us, anger creeps out, and as our reactions becomes louder, reaction times get shorter. We are not as effective as we need to be to navigate our situations, and we may need additional help. Overly identifying with our emotional states and ineffective ways of expressing our dismay can be warning signs that we need new coping mechanisms. Talking to a trained professional can help you think about the life you want in a different way than you are living now, if it feels like too much.

People have a need to be seen, heard, and accepted. It should begin at the original home, but if it does not, I hope there is a teacher or grandparent who is able to listen and not judge. Teach children to be kind to themselves so they know how to be kind to others. Allowing children to express themselves without condemnation teaches them to emote and helps them go through the process of feeling, coping, and soothing themselves. When we deny them that dance, it carries into adulthood the need to walk away from the discomfort of feeling. Feeling is programmed in us. Denying that creates havoc on our internal life and bleeds out into our relationships.

My beautiful granddaughter taught me a valuable lesson about speaking up for myself. During Halloween season, she was experimenting with being a bold cheerleader for a school project. The first line she came up with was, "I am not your prop." At eleven, she understood and expressed she was not allowing anyone to define her or dictate how she should be.

Cultural and societal norms should not usurp our humanness. Some seventy years ago, there was a norm, even a law, against interracial and same-sex marriages in the United States. Who has the right to stop people from loving each other? Surely no government body. No human should deny love to flourish in our hearts and being.

How many times in a week do you say, "in my family," or "my mother said," or "my father taught me," things, such as not to show emotions? Why do we hold so deeply to those early days when, as adults, we notice that belief could use some editing? If those familial norms no longer suit the real essence of who you are, upgrade your thoughts to a belief that honors your essence and sense of well-being.

Why do we exalt our family's behavior over another's family? How do we free our minds to reshape our separate families into a shared life with others who may have been brought up differently? Create your own family beliefs based on love and respect for each other rather than focusing on your different upbringings.

My coaching client, Jill, said she hasn't trusted her husband in a long while. She recounted that she hadn't trusted her well-being had a place in her first or her second husband's hands. She admitted she had become an untrusting person, and it was hellish in her mind. Jill didn't start marriages with mistrust. She had to trace back to when she felt unsafe trusting people. She went on to examine when she stopped trusting herself to love freely; without her pattern to demand safety from men rather than safety with herself.

As she took small steps toward trusting herself, she could affirm her rightful place in relationship with men. Her goals became feeling safe with herself and others. To do this, she had to change her perception. Then, she could watch that change her circumstances. That's the power of seeing and feeling emotions to evoke change. Change happens when we are resilient, not when we give up.

By living in Love, we find our creativity and ways to be resilient. We can see through Love's light. That light is filled with creative energy and solutions—graciously, excitedly, expectantly—that is our individual right. Our responsibility is to community, creating space in which to work together. Individualism versus community doesn't work for our overall good. Individual gifts shared help the world community.

My own need for wholeness included self-acceptance of my beautiful aspects as well as my uglier ways. Accepting my personal bumps and bruises allowed me to drop others' ideas of what I should do and be if their point of view did not serve my quest to be a whole, functioning person. It also created an opening not to fear the saddest emotions and loftiest desires and cravings. In that opening, I could feel the pain from yesteryear and apply the kind of forgiveness that would free me from having to carry judgment that can stop love circulating through me. My relationship with myself extends to how I think of myself, how I feel about myself, and how I believe foundationally in something larger than myself.

Chapter Three

Powerful and Positive
Thinking

W hat is your perception of yourself? To get to that answer you
must be willing to observe how you think about yourself and
how you speak aloud about yourself to trusted others. I dare say a lot
of people will think some version of: *I could be a better person*.

Another word for this might be *unworthiness*. You may feel you are
not deserving of love or acceptance because you believe yourself to be
lacking, or you believe you are not who you should be. I challenge you
to try on new thoughts about yourself and wear them around for a while.

Practice saying quietly to yourself thoughts that stir your self-beliefs
into new territory, sentiments such as: *My holiness is my commitment to
happiness*, or *My contentment is my holiness that becomes my joy in living*. See
holiness as a substance that cleans our slate of misdeeds, so we may be
and do better toward ourselves. Holiness is our recognition that we
are whole at birth. Get acquainted with the self you were meant to be.

Mind Shift — Who You Were Meant to Be

There is no need to be afraid of the word *holiness*. I am not talking about a religious deity or ideal that seems too lofty and outside our human ability. I am suggesting you get in touch with your best and highest version of yourself.

Start with your acceptance of there being a better version of yourself who has been hiding behind unkind thoughts. Adopt the desire to recognize the higher version of yourself you were meant to express because the world needs your best-operating self.

Start with a sheet of paper and writing instrument. On one side of the sheet, list your strengths. Everyone has some strengths, so stop saying you don't have any. Also add the secret attributes and aspects you would like to develop and share with no fear of judgment.

On the other side of the sheet, list the thoughts about yourself you repeat daily that hold you back from being who you are meant to express.

You know the ones:
- *I'm too old to change.*
- *I never have been good at* (fill in the blank).
- *I'm too tired to change.*
- *No one will believe me.*

List whatever words block your mind from the belief that you are more than you have allowed yourself to be.

Use this work to become aware of where or how you diminish yourself. In this chapter, you build ways and habits that improve your mental vision into clearer thinking.

Personal Thinking

Let's get into how we think things through. Thoughts are created from perceptions that can become cemented beliefs, likely created from our past acts and interactions. Perceptions can be changed. I know this to be true because each of us has perceptions, and where multitudes exist, there lies a pathway to other ideas. These perceptions can determine the importance or unimportance of what is said or done around us.

A glass of water is important if we are thirsty and unimportant if we are not. You might see the glass as a useful tool, or if you were injured when young by broken glass, you might see it as a dangerous weapon. What has happened to you can matter or not; it's your decision entirely. Just remember, if you base your perception of glass on experiences that negate all the times it was harmless, you limit yourself from using all types of glassware, metaphorically speaking.

People believe their thoughts are their truth, but thoughts are just thoughts. Thoughts have weight only if you give them power. How have your thoughts about yourself helped you grow into the person you want to be? Your thoughts do not have to take you down a spiraling snake hole. Your thoughts—the stories you tell yourself—become self-fulfilling belief systems. As you co-create your beliefs, you co-create your life. When you are in situations that create stress or that trigger you, challenge yourself to think differently concerning the situation. Practice thinking outside the box you have built around yourself.

Our thoughts can produce either heavenly or hellishly painful outcomes. It is my decision which thoughts I hold. When I think lovingly, I may not have any conscious knowledge of the miracles I invoke in my life or the lives of others. You may find out at a later time of the miracles connected to your thoughts. You may not discover any at all; however, it does not mean a miracle has not happened.

A disciplined, positive mind creates more peace-filled experiences. An undisciplined mind creates the havoc of scattered litter swirling in a wind tunnel, pulling your emotions from one fear-based thought to another throughout your day. Discipline is about choice. To choose wisely is to accept joy and love as your leading guideposts. Build a foundational story—thoughts—on loving and having joy in your life. A wisdom-thinking foundation helps you when life takes unexpected turns.

Foundational Belief Setting

Setting foundational beliefs starts with having faith in positive energy and opening to let the Universe's Energy conspire with you for your highest good. Foundational beliefs offer inspiring words you can sit upon when you are feeling weak. They create connection to something greater than yourself. They are a foundation of positive energy you can stand, lean, and lie on during the hardest of times. We all have experienced difficult moments in our lives.

To set your own Foundation, truthfully examine your beliefs in various aspects of your life: 1) Relationships, with yourself and with others; 2) Well-being, both financial and physical; and 3) Spirituality and sense of purpose.

1. Start with one at a time. For each category, indicate the foundational beliefs you stand on today. Not sure what they are? Take a peek into any category and identify what is happening in that aspect of your life.

2. After you have completed writing about all the areas, identify the broad similarities.
    That's what you believe in this moment.

3. Sit with the information for a few minutes and make no judgment. Let's use relationships as a sample.

Starting with self, you may have written:
I am off-balance when talking to others. I am tired of not speaking up. I am tired of not being seen, heard, or supported.

4. Next, focus on those others in your life and list what you tell yourself about your interactions with them.
   It may look like this: *People are critical and dismissive of me. My relationships with others are not great. The majority of the people I am around are not trustworthy when I want to share my emotions.*
   With that combined assessment, you could summarize that your interactions in relationships are difficult. That is a current foundational belief likely developed over a long period.

5. Self-reflection is the next step. Ask yourself the following questions:
   Is that what I want to continue to believe?
   Will holding on to that old belief create an opening for better relationship experiences?
   If the answers are no, then ask yourself:
   How do I want to feel about relationships?
   What needs to be revised in my thinking to get to that new belief?

6. Entertain how you want to feel and how your beliefs need to be revised to get to that new state you desire. Write it all down. Nothing is wrong and there is no need to be *perfect*. Combining two answers could give you a closer-to-perfect answer. Be open to what is best for you. Get still in your mind and body. Open your mind and desire to new awareness on how to think of relationships. Here's a sample statement of new awareness:
   Relationships require honesty that is said in a loving way, starting with myself.

7. Your statement becomes a belief with practice. Over time with consistent awareness, you can live in alignment with your new desires, holding desires close, but not too tightly. Detach from specific outcomes. Applaud every recognizable improvement,

no matter how small or tall. Dismiss without cruelty to yourself any regressions. If you slip, quickly apologize to yourself for any harshness you spewed toward yourself. Remember you are working toward an improved practice that becomes your solid foundation.

I recommend questioning yourself because that becomes a pathway to self-understanding, and it is a vital commitment to more thoughtful thinking. We have a responsibility to investigate our thinking that built our current belief foundation and may or may not serve our highest good. You have dominant thoughts that have ruled your life and held you back. As you recognize your repetitive thoughts, question their origin and validity for the life you desire.

Here are sample questions you may add to as your own come up:

- *Is that thought true? According to whom?*
- *Who are the people who told me this is the way to think?*
- *What happened in their life to make them think that way?*
- *What incidents happened to support me thinking this way?*
- *Were there extenuating circumstances that created the very thoughts I am holding on to that no longer serve me well?*

Why have you held so tightly to those un-serving thoughts? Our nature is to want to be right, which can cause us to hold on to versions of who we think we should be or who our families demand us to be, even when we are not thrilled with who we are pretending to be.

To help navigate difficulties with courage and perseverance, envision a higher version of yourself. That is how to live powerfully and with purpose. How we think creates how we feel. How we feel affects our day's interactions internally with ourselves and externally with others.

If you are unsure how to evolve and you feel unsteady about your next steps, look to your subconscious for guidance, especially at night, just before drifting off to sleep. Ask your subconscious to send you answers about what happened and why you think and feel this way. This will allow you to get on with your purpose-driven desires. It may give you glimpses into your past, such as discovering what you heard about yourself as a younger person.

At the center of my foundational belief is *God is my Source*. Surrounding that statement are other phrases, such as:

- Live in the present moment
- Love and be loved
- Inspire others
- Be fearless
- Be curious
- Listen

These and a few other statements have served me well. I have not needed to change this list in the last few years; however, when I first created it, I tweaked it several times to represent the beliefs I can stand on in good and difficult times.

We can work on ourselves and go along for some time thinking and feeling balanced. Then life throws us a curveball, and we may have to reach deeper to regroup, as our purpose can shift. The distress of doing that which is not your purpose—not your loving expression—creates a disconnect with your energetic body and affects your thoughts about yourself and others. You think your job isn't fulfilling, but you must pay bills. You believe your purpose can't pay the bills, and your job and family eat up your time and energy. Your body breaks down; your mental acuity suffers. You try to hide the defect from others, which becomes another separation, producing more stress. You keep reaching for new thinking connections, examining how you want to feel and what you want to experience.

Sometimes, we think obligations impede thinking for ourselves and living purposefully. Obligations are real, and they are as real as our purpose. Look for ways to combine your talents. The first ten years of my adult working life, I didn't identify I was using my gifts when I helped the people who naturally gravitated to me for advice or counsel. I was a recruiter for a financial institution, and the people to whom I extended offers of employment would find reasons to see me and ask for lunch dates or meetings in my office, allowing us to talk for longer periods. Typically, the recruiter is the facilitator and doesn't continue to work with the newly hired after their start date, unless of course, they are managers who need new employees hired. My gift, let's call it *my purpose*, brought them back to me. Your gift is likely something that comes so easily to you, you discount it, thinking anyone can do it if you can.

What is your innate gift?

What compliments do people give you that you have dismissed?

For example, I have an intuitive ability to see people, not only as who they are, but also in their possibility. I sense their mental hurts and energetic wounds. I don't always know the specific details, although there are times when my inner knowing guidance whispers that I should ask a specific question.

I created space for those potential new hires to feel seen and heard and cared about. They could lay down their walls and shed their personal armor, sharing themselves without feeling judged or worried. I asked thoughtful questions, and fortunately, they could feel comfortable sharing their true selves rather than their imagined, acceptable selves. I was not conscious of my gift; I simply felt the human connection. I felt lighter because in my small way, I helped someone get a job. In other cases, the hiring manager or I saved others from the agony of securing the wrong job by not hiring them.

Here's another lesson I picked up later in my corporate career: My deepest desire was to be an author. Little did I know the jobs I worked at were providing lessons I could write about many years later to demonstrate how life can work to our advantage. I was not aware in those early working years that I was honing my coaching and writing skills. So many years passed during which I whined to my friends: *I want to be a writer.* They were encouraging and I was fearful.

My thinking was fraught with concerns about my ability to reach others. I trusted neither myself nor the Universe in those early years. I used what I perceived as valid excuses: *I am a wife; I am a mother; I am an employee; I am a daughter.* I hope you caught the phrase "*perceived as valid excuses*" because that's what they were. Catch the limits as well that I placed on myself by the labels I used. When you say *I am* . . . watch that it is not simply an excuse to avoid what you really want to accomplish.

I bought journals and in them I tried to write, mimicking famous and favorite authors. I would watch interviews of the authors, trying to get a glimpse into how they accomplished all they did. I learned from Toni Morrison that you write, and then you edit, and then you edit again and again. I learned from Iyanla Vansant you speak in your own voice—no need to mimic anyone else because each of us has a unique life and lessons to share.

I wrote about my thoughts, feelings, and emotional bruises and dug deep to use my voice and my highest thinking at each junction. That was my work to do and my responsibility.

No one else can do your work for you to get clearer about who you are and what you want. Your examination of yourself becomes clearer. Be nonjudgmental while hearing what is truly important to the inner you. Do not squash ideas. Write what you hear and walk around with it to see what becomes louder:

- Does anything need healing?
- Are you guided to make changes?

Take responsibility for the life you have created with your thinking capabilities. To choose wisely is to take personal responsibility for who you are. Note how you open your energy channels for where you want to go and how you choose to be. Start with your inside thinking life and observe as you heal.

While your thinking evolves, what you say and do change externally to support your best self in your daily living. When our awakened self leads, we can be kind to others and set boundaries that were not apparent before our inner work was done. Mental work includes boundary setting, while the lack of boundaries feels twisted, like a pretzel. Boundaries that support your well-being give you energy to love yourself and to help others. Folks who are givers without boundaries can become curt with people and may feel unappreciated. Strive for your thinking to become your safe place.

Join your mental forces with positive power rather than perpetually painful thoughts. Choose loving thoughts, forgiveness, and faith in a rewarding life. The power of choice is in your control. Choose freedom to choose yourself. Choose joy by replacing runaway, limited ego-thoughts with an identity of intentional joy.

When I'm choosing wisely, I look at people's behavior. Either it's loving or it's crying out for love, a principle I learned studying *A Course in Miracles* (Foundation for Inner Peace, 1975). I must monitor my perception of things said to me and know my thoughts can lead to judgment of people surrounding me. But my judgment of people's behavior toward me requires me to choose wisely, not wildly. *Choose compassionately* is my first thought. I have learned it does not require me to stay in the presence of behavior or words that are intentionally harmful. I can pray for people whose behavior is crying out for help and let them go on their path, I hope, to find their best self.

I am also careful to check in with myself: What is in me and my thinking or feeling that is upset? What do I need to discover or heal within me? Thinking it through frees me from holding on to the illusion of hurt. It allows me to sustain compassion toward myself and others.

Another aspect of perceived misalignment is when things change, and we say: *I feel powerless and I want to give up*. Life changes to move us to the next higher level of being and realization. Begin to trust that change is inevitable. Free yourself from holding tightly to thoughts of change that create fear, discord, or angst.

A possible response when life feels out of alignment is: *What are you here to teach me?*

When illness developed while I was writing my first book, it was helpful. I lost sight in my left eye for three months. Not only did I lose my sight, but also I felt physical pain. Light of any kind made my eye hurt. If I moved my head, there would be a piercing pain, and no drugs could help me through it.

Through this experience, I learned to ask for help. This was difficult because I had been learning self-sufficiency since age seven. My mother worked outside the home. I would open the door after school with my own key—the term then was *latchkey kid*. I was responsible for calling her at work to say I was home, changing into my play clothes, putting away my school clothes, doing homework, and always cleaning up after myself before I watched television. Because I was an only child, self-sufficiency was my way of not being a bother. So how did I change from self-sufficiency to asking for help? I changed my mind and broadened my perception of receiving and accepted the opportunity for growth.

The only thoughts I entertained during my sight loss were:

- *I will see again, and I will see well.*
- *I will be free of pain.*
- *I trust the Universe, my God-Source energy to bring this forth.*

It took three months before some semblance of sight returned. So many things had to change because in certain light, I couldn't see words clearly. I couldn't find the cursor on my computer; this was before accessibility, whereas now we are able to make the cursor much larger. I had to dim the lights in my office when I returned to work. If a clear or white object was placed on a white surface, I couldn't distinguish it. My brain and my eyes didn't work together well, so I could see a picture and miss major parts of it. I could have thought of these circumstances as devastating, since I consider myself a hobby photographer.

But remember, my resolve was: *I will see again, and I will see well.* It was a slow return to seeing clearly, but my thoughts about seeing again became my reality. I believed in the possibility more strongly than I believed in what was happening in that temporary moment. On reflection, I wanted to understand why this needed to happen. I was writing my first book, a dream since freshman English class in college.

Did I not want to see the book to fruition?

Did I not want to observe the possibilities the book might have created?

Neither. Instead, I had to realize that asking for help was not a sign of weakness. I should have known this, since I listened to and offered help to others, never thinking anyone was weak. My helping is always an act of kindness. People who love me just wanted to offer me their kindness, and I learned to accept it in gratitude and trust. Friends proofread my manuscript, wrote notes back to the editor for me, and supported my vision that I would see clearly once again.

Thoughts that run in our mind are not solid; therefore, you can stop holding any thought as if it is your absolute truth. Thoughts can come and go; however, we get in trouble when we think they are real. In this situation, the definition of suffering is believing in any repetitive thoughts that create a reality you do not want. I call it *mental immaturity* when we allow thoughts to run wild in our mind. For my coaching clients who don't like that term, I use *mental congestion* to be gentle.

Mental congestion is the inability to decide to think differently, to get out of your own distorted way of thinking and believe situations and circumstances that no longer serve a genuine loving purpose. If you can't choose your purpose or a meaningful destination, you remain stuck and a foreigner to your true self and your authentic desires. Mental congestion is that back-and-forth *I'm going to do this; no, I'm not capable. I want this, but "they" won't let me get it.*

Mental immaturity is letting your mind constantly wander into territory of unkindness in thoughts about yourself and others. Runaway thoughts keep you falling into mental dugouts of sadness and angst that allow you to believe there is something inherently flawed about yourself. Mental immaturity takes us away from our conscious truth of who we truly are: a beacon of light, love, and joy. We are meant to be living in a greater sense of inner peace, no matter the broken-wing situations we have encountered along the journey of our life. A broken wing is any burden you carry that becomes too heavy, such as past traumas: death of a loved one, extreme mistreatment, or tragic events. Allow that broken wing to create space for more faith, not fear and not frustration. Fear and its by-product, frustration, block new possibilities, which are our birthright.

Our target is mental maturity. How do we achieve mental maturity over thoughts of despair and self-degradation? When a thought has persisted since you were a young person, try one of the following two statements:

- *That is no longer true.*

or

- *Stop! I am canceling that thought because it does not serve me well in my life today.*

The shift begins when you decide to disavow the old thinking with the statements above or one that resonates with your particular circumstance. As you consistently address the persistently unhelpful thought, notice that your voice takes on an authoritative and self-assured tone. After you command *Stop!* to the unhelpful, repetitive thought, you train your brain with supportive, affirming thoughts you would rather have, starting today.

For example, if you are a person who says or believes fundamentally that you can't trust people, you may be thinking and telling a few close friends, "I am always disappointed by people." In your heart, however, you are yearning for a trusting connection. To work on a mental teardown of beliefs and thoughts that do not support your true desire, replace the old rampant thoughts with new and supportive thought-language, such as:

I trust myself to surround myself with supportive people.

I attract people who are supportive.

For further growth, you may find it helpful to examine your observations about relationships while growing up. Challenge yourself to let go the old frame of reference to gain a better, brighter reality. The regrets of the past keep us confused, and when we are off-balance, discerning the right thing to do in the current moment is difficult. Just because we saw behaviors in our early years, they don't have to continue, nor do they need to be the narrative of our adult years.

Mind Shift: Awareness Breathing Creates (ABC)

If, when you are driving around in your car or shopping for groceries or at work, you find yourself frightened about memories you are not sure have happened or how they came to be, ground yourself in the present moment. You have no proof or evidence in this moment that what happened is occurring right now.

Breathe deeply, which helps to put you in this moment. If the fear coming up relates to something that happened in your past, you are breathing yourself back to the present moment.

In the present moment, you are safe, and again, you have no proof the fear of your thought is true. If it proves true, trust that you have the ability to handle it, and afford yourself adequate breath to help you to do so. When it proves not to be true, be grateful you didn't spend hours worrying when there was nothing to worry about.

This exercise is helpful when you have allowed the past to interrupt your present moments. Breathing awareness soothes the brain and the heart centers, thereby returning you safely and gently to the present moment.

This is how you can represent your brightness in life, not the darkness of the long ago past.

The Highest Energy Force created you and you can make space for that energy to come through you in your ABC practice. Our Highest Energy radiates our brightest light. That's us being humble, not arrogant.

This practice centers you to give as good as what you are craving from others. Repeat breathing in and out, deeply into the diaphragm. Watch or feel your stomach protrude as you breath in and contract toward your backbone as you breath out. Allow the repetitions to center you and relieve the frightful memories to their rightful place, in the past.

The past is gone; it is only awake in our memory, and we allow its interruption when we stay focused on the memory and the pain. Our future may or may not be predictable. Our present is here to be appreciated and to be enjoyed, not to be recreated in a perpetually recurring thought of the past cycle.

As you embrace present joy, you open the brain's pathways to continue experiencing joy. The pervasive darkness you have known can be laid to rest. Be wary of the critical thoughts that return, even louder, to strengthen the ego. Your ego is trying to protect you, but the reality is it creates personal suffering and feelings of unworthiness. The ego's hold can be released when you understand that guilt, harsh warnings, and fear of the unknown need not rule you any longer.

Thoughts are a construction project designed by others to control you and hold you back from living your purposeful life. Break free of them by declining to revisit the past transgressions in your mind. Break the connection to stop the repetition. Accept this fact: if you focus on what happened before—on what you were taught, what you perceived, or what you experienced—you are calling it into your present and, therefore, possibly setting up your future in the same unhappy way. Let go the thoughts of the way it worked in the past. Embrace the present with a healthy new mental attitude that trusts a free future provided by your innate intelligence from your Energy Source that desires your very best life.

Lay down the hurtful past. Embrace the present with a happy heart and trust in a Divine future. That translates to laying down your burdens, shortcomings, guilt, and shame. Say goodbye to thoughts that hold you down or hold you back from your positive movement. Identify and reframe the repetitive thoughts that have held you captive.

To lay them down, you must make peace with what happened by trusting it happened to help you learn lessons that led you to a personal journey that can now assist others by example, through encouragement, self-acceptance, and therefore personal forgiveness that leads you and others into mental and emotional freedom.

You don't have to do this alone—therapists, life coaches, and mentors can be good listeners and offer thoughtful questions—but it's imperative you understand the answers are *within you*. Your personal journey is your responsibility. It does not belong to anyone else. Thank your internal guidance for assistance, words, and awareness that it is from on High, and therefore, is good!

When we allow persistent thoughts, we must accept that our minds will be scattered. We have the ability with practice to actively deny old power-play thoughts. Mental immaturity is apparent when our thoughts are allowed—by us—to be undisciplined. We are responsible for our own thinking.

Our experiences can be the effects of our thinking, which I refer to as *cause and effect*. Irrational anxiety-thinking requires examination. Now that you are an adult, no one is making you think what you are thinking. It's all on you to decide which thoughts you let linger and which you dismiss. Build your mental muscles in ways and ideas that guide you to willingly see things differently. That is your responsibility to yourself. Trust yourself and your Divine Intuition. You take that energy and ability with you wherever you go, much like a spirit warrior.

I enjoy taking walks along our tree-lined city streets to connect with my Divine Intuition in the energy of nature. I make the declaration on my walks to focus on ideas that uplift me. Ideas such as: *I desire to live a happy life*. This shifts my energy into feeling happy. I admire whatever condition the trees are in, and that phase of observation shifts me. I do not judge where the tree is or how the tree looks. They all have stages of beauty throughout each season, and that puts me into a happiness phase. I put no stock in the notion that trees must be in full bloom. I can admire the stage of leafless trees; even dying trees have a beauty to them. I declare peace within myself just looking up at the sky. I admire the clouds and the in-and-out showing of the sun. Nature is a reminder; things change, so I enjoy what is in front of me right now. The weather pattern changes and settles back down, just like our lives.

What can you do that puts you in an uplifted frame of mind?

You can set an intention for your desire, which becomes the cause for the effects. Pay particular attention to what you say during intention setting. I often remind people to say what you mean and mean what you say. Some people declare what they want while speaking aloud the opposite of what they said they want. For example, if someone says, "I want a good job," in one sentence, and in the next breath they say, "Of course there are no good jobs or good companies anymore." The effect is shown in the response they give to not getting what they desired: "See? Declaring isn't working," they'll say.

They are totally missing the point that each of us has the personal power to choose our way of thinking and thereby to design the life of our desires and dreams. Watch thoughtfully: What you say may contradict what you truly want. New ways of thinking help energy to shift toward your desire. Whether your energy shifts depend on what you're thinking and saying.

Build your words with integrity. Be clear about your intention and identify the experience you desire. Know your reason for seeking the experience you desire. If you are brave enough, allow your wildest dreams to be the first act of your intention planning. Combine your intention with your purpose, and go for it.

Mind Shift: Intention Setting

Write a list of intention sentences that can encourage you.

Here are a couple of examples to prime your brain for new thoughts and beginnings:

My intention creates my reality.

Either I stand by my intention, or I default on my desires.

Once you have defined your intention, use a repetitive tool to keep you focused. I recommend using a strand of beads to repeat an intention-setting, positive quote. These beads are called *mala* (108 beads), *rosary* (59 beads), or *subha* (99 beads) and have been in use since at least the eighth century by people meditating and reciting prayer.

They are used by people in many religious faiths—including Hindu, Buddhist, Catholic, and Muslim—to focus the mind, to strengthen mental health, to deepen spiritual awareness, and to cultivate mindfulness. The more secular benefits touted are reducing stress and improving our cognitive abilities.

Hindus consider 108 a sacred number. Some say the number one represents the Supreme Being of Creation and your highest good. Zero represents our humanity with no need for our ego-voice. Eight represents the infinity symbol, our relationship to our eternity.

As a young girl, I was first introduced to contemplations with the beads in the Catholic church tradition. Later I learned to use them during yoga and meditation practices. Some people wear their beads when not in use as a necklace or wrapped around the arm as a bracelet. Some strands consist of gems chosen for their various energetic properties.

When I use my mala beads, I can sense evidence of the energetic shift that happens within me. I start by saying one mantra for each bead my fingers touch along the strand. I observe the speed with which I'm saying the words. If I am going too fast or too slowly, I vary the speed. If I am in a space where I may disturb others, I'll whisper or repeat the prayer or mantra silently.

Have the exercises of working with the beads worked every time? Not necessarily in the beginning. Once I was unable to forgive myself for not being open to someone else's innocence. This is one of the few times that the mala bead exercise didn't alleviate my unhappiness. It let me know I had more salvation-searching to do, as I was connecting with my immature mind and heart space. I became grateful that I could see the error of my way and understand in that scenario, self-forgiveness was to be my freedom.

Early in the process, the shift into peaceful feelings took nearly the entire strand. Now I shift and notice a smile before I am quarter of the way in. I keep going to set the tone within my mind and body for the rest of the day. When I wake up feeling sad, unhappy thoughts flood the room's energy. In despair, I grab my mala and watch with a smile and a deep conviction in my voice how serenity resurfaces. I declare that my intention is to have a good day. There is power in giving myself over to an omnipotent energy.

By the time I finish my 108 affirmations, I am once again ignited. I can again feel the greatness that is both personal and worldly. I can accept myself and that God is my Source, my love, and it's my purpose to share that love.

As you become familiar with the process, you can use your intention-specific statements on all the beads regularly. Examples to get you started are listed below. You can create your own based on the important nudge you are hiding.

I am secure there is a happy outcome.

Peace and joy are my foundation.

I am the creator of my truth.

You are the curator of your thoughts. If your thoughts are creating unhappiness or dis-ease within yourself, then you can curate higher thoughts that bring you to the bull's eye, your center of calm. It requires you to think differently. You can create what you think; therefore, you have the internal power to think and see things differently. Take away the power of the haunting doomsday of repetitive thinking and replace it with supporting thoughts, if you want to accept yourself, love yourself, and be less anxious.

Whatever is plaguing you, decide first that you want to change. Secondly, let go of the fear that the world will crumble if you change your mind and, therefore, your behavior. You will survive, and you deserve a life with more joy and love for self and compassion for others. That's the freedom way to live your highest and best life for you and those around you.

In order to invoke change, you have to become so tired—tired of being tired, I like to say—of thought patterns that keep you living in mistrust, conflict, and combative mind messages focused on the past and the future that obstruct the present moment. You can practice how to experience space between your thoughts.

When was the last time you let your mind relax?

When was the last time your body felt relaxed?

Your mind and your body are the two instruments that create your existence. they deserve rest and care, and if you don't give those to yourself, who will? No one can know what is best for you. They can guess or assume, but they cannot know what is in your heart. They cannot know what you came to Earth to do. They can pontificate; they can try to persuade, but only you know the truth of who you are. The Truth can be buried, and that can make you feel uncertain, but the information was programmed in you at birth. You likely knew your Truth as a child. If you can't recall it today in adulthood, it may have been scolded out of you or ignored.

When we live believing our first awareness in life is to accept our parents as all-knowing, we make decisions unconsciously. How many times have you said to someone: "Because that's the way I was raised"? Rather than acknowledging, as adults, we are on Earth to learn our individual lessons. If that's true, can we look inward and separate our lessons from our parents' lessons and examine whether our beliefs are the same? If you discover your beliefs are different, work on your self-acceptance and understand your family has their own right to disagree.

What is your ultimate lesson from believing your parents' beliefs?

Human parents and guardians have human flaws. We are God's creations. Why wouldn't the Creator want all that is good for us? We are hopeful our human guardians see, accept, and support us. However, we must remember that they carry their hurts and pain in front of them and try to protect us from beliefs they have carried most of their lives. Some parents try to toughen us to prepare us for a world they perceive as harsh. Some try to cushion us from the harrowing life they perceived ahead and outside our home. I contend parents have done the best they can, given the human experiences they have had.

Now that you are an adult, you can question and examine what is right for you and what creates your joy. How about this as an ultimate truth: God loves you and your parents. You are His Creation and He wants you to be joyful and to create a better life of caring and loving yourself that then feels natural to extend to others. This understanding can lead to feelings of freeness and abundance.

You are no longer prisoner to an ill-fitting, old formula of asking others for permission while denying your wants, needs, and desires. Not that we all were even conscious of the ill fit; some of us put our guardians on a pedestal. We believed them to be all-knowing. We were taught that questioning them was disrespectful.

I wonder if you are experiencing fits of anger and rage that come up for you unexpectedly. When we deny other people trying to control us and dampen our spirits, we have to wonder how that disappointment is evident in our lives. Ask yourself:

- *What is this incident teaching me?*
- *Where does my overreaction stem from?*
- *Why the need to comfort myself with addictions that aren't good for me?*
- *What am I trying to soothe?*
- *Why am I uncomfortable with myself and other people who don't think like or look like me or my family?*

You could be reacting to your past memories and the beliefs of your family. I'm not angry with parents or caretakers anymore. I believe each one did their best with what they knew, based on past experiences, just as we do. Our personal revolution to thinking freely is not against them. You can examine what you were taught and your individual ideas for your personal growth. It could be a fundamental change from what you were taught to what you know is inherently true for you. You pick the type of people you want to befriend and whom you are allowed to love. You return to your ultimate, great, and powerful self and watch your thinking and speaking so they are congruent with your heart space.

Who Defines You

Beyond the family structure is interaction with the outside world. The treatment received outside your home can affect your mind, heart, and feelings. Marginalization is treatment that makes perceived *others* feel insignificant and dehumanized by perceived people in power. Marginalization is inflicted toward people who are not being seen, heard, and certainly not being appreciated.

Some Black women tell me they walk down a city street and are bumped into by people at alarming rates, as if they are invisible to other walkers. When you look different from most people in the room at school or work and you say something, but your comment is not recognized, that sets up the energy in the room to ignore the person who looks different. Notice I used the words *not recognized* because when I was that person, I knew people could hear me in meetings. Especially when someone else in the room would say my exact words a few minutes later. My band of women friends at work consciously decided that when a women's voice was being ignored, other women would say: "as Deborah said, earlier . . ." And as I grew into my freer self, I began thanking men for repeating exactly what I had just said. No one did that twice.

Other modern-day oppressive subtleties are inflicted regularly. When a person of color is terminated from a position, chances are the manager will not hire another for the same position. Whereas when a manager fires a majority person, it is customarily understood that it was just the wrong fit, not that an entire race is wrong.

I had to fight for extremely obese people to be hired and promoted to leadership positions amid horrible jokes spoken by hiring managers. But I fought for their knowledge and right to be there. Most, I am proud to say, were promoted to higher positions and became long-term and well-respected employees.

If we work in a place that doesn't feel safe emotionally, we can live in a fear-based state and feel stressed. Worrying about getting our work done so we can feed our family adds pressure to our adrenal system. We shut down from constant anxiety, which negatively impacts our immune system, robbing us of the energy we need to live a healthy and smart existence.

People handle the atrocities of marginalization in many ways once they are aware it is happening. Some people drink a little more after work to take the edge off. Some people will galvanize and organize to take to the streets to protest. My first go-to remedy is to take a personal assessment of my mental state and self-perception improvement and to extend some grace. I assess whether am I feeling self-assured when I speak up.

- *What comes across in my voice and mannerisms?*
- *Am I making eye contact?*
- *Am I being clear?*
- *Is there anything I can do differently going forward to garner what I need?*

I decide to accept my best and most-assured self.

We can no longer afford to let others define us by their standards alone. The definitions of cultural institutions—government representatives, institutions, educational and religious ideologies, neighborhood norms, family preferences, work environments—promote conformity, which creates individual angst, personal and cultural malaise, dishonesty, hiding, and coverup.

Check in with yourself and ask:

- *Am I holding back, believing in the subtleties I experience in the world around me?*
- *Am I hiding my brilliance from the people I have grown up with?*

We are here to live our lives with dignity and take our greatness wherever we go. If yours is not appreciated, you have the right to go where you are seen and heard and accepted. If you choose not to leave, then you need to find ways that are healthy and affirming to release your stress. You see beyond the limits being placed upon you. It is your responsibility to care for your mental and emotional health. Start by not believing the oppressors' messages. These may take the form of limits placed on you, toxic culture, racism, lack of respect, or a generally unhealthy vibe. You may notice aggressions and preconceived notions your colleagues bring to the work environment.

Whatever the behavior or feeling, these questions must be asked:
- Is it the corporate culture or is it the people working there?
- Is it the government or is it the people?
- Is it the Supreme Court or is it the people?

The concepts of individualism as well as *live and let live* create fear among those who need conformity to appear powerful. But what they do in the dark can be seen when we shine our mental light on their hypocrisy.

Racism, ableism, sexism, and all the other -isms are used to exclude. Marginalization is a ploy to keep you stuck in the place someone else wants to keep you in. They say and do things to convince you and others that you are less qualified or less effective than you perceive yourself to be.

The way out of playing into their imagination is to think for yourself and advocate for your special gifts. Pull the curtains back on their agenda; grab the curtain cord to adjust the light. Shine additionally needed light on the situation, and thereby increase your energy to get the job done. When you take responsibility for your own well-being and your desire to shine your authentic light, the reason others do what they do to corrupt the system in their favor does not matter. We do not put our spark in anyone else's hands for safekeeping. You honor your gifts and use them where they are needed and appreciated.

Marginalizers can smell our need to be liked, to be thought well of, and to be appreciated. They will give you platitudes and little bites but will yank the floor out from under you. When you are in your authentic strength they may try once, but not again. Remember the playground, where bullies pushed the perceived weakest kid? It continued until the so-called weakest kid stood up for themself. Then the bullying game was over.

One of my gifts is seeing all sides of a matter; another is seeing the past and its effect on the present and the future. These are helpful for breaking *barricade thinking*, which holds us back from being our best and brightest selves. I have come to understand that no one can make you as an individual feel *less than* unless you believe it and act as though your lack of worth is true. Notice I did not say *powerful* or *smart*, because the truth of the matter is you are likely both, and that is what frightens people into applying social exclusion. If your like group is being blocked from promotion, and everyone in your group can see it and feel it, they can commiserate with you. That's what the powerbrokers want: they want you to feel defeated and to work harder but get nowhere fast.

Here's the message: You control how you feel.

You must oversee what you think. It's your mental maturity working for you. Thinking: *They won't let me in* diminishes your personal power. Frankly, what they are saying just is not true. The powerbrokers have their own insecurities and fear factors and self-judgments. You just can't see them because you are too caught up in their vison of you.

Think about a friend who is visibly upset about something someone said. You don't understand why they are upset about the infraction, but you are a supportive friend. If you have experienced similar emotions or situations, you could likely empathize with and understand their being shaken. If you have no experience like this, it may be harder to understand why your friend is so upset.

Let's take this scenario a step further. The people your friend works with will not let them into a board meeting. Perhaps through conditioning, your friend feels somewhere deep inside there is a grain of truth that something within them is lacking. This keeps them from being included—from allowing themself to be included. We can see how that thinking may be part of their upset.

If your friend did not believe something was inherently wrong with them, they may not have been as deeply affected by the slight. Invite your friend to consider this is a gift, an opportunity to dig into their past, to uncover when they heard this before and the feelings it inspires. They can work on healing that infraction to move beyond the hurt coming up today. They can also make new decisions, asking for what they deserve, seeking places that see and welcome their genius.

Let's not focus only on work environments. This dynamic also occurs in families, schools, extracurricular activities, and even religious institutions. It may appear as human nature preserving its own; however, I would weigh in on other possibilities. Perhaps when one exerts power over another, it is because of their own sense of lack—a need to feel superior because they lack their own feelings of self-love. Maybe it wasn't shown or taught in their earlier situations. I've worked with numerous power leaders who shared a sense while growing up that their parents thought they would not amount to any high social standard—as if that is the only marker for success.

Well, they made it to the perceived top and were still unsure of themselves; some were fearful of losing it all in an instant. Many senior managers do not embrace their personal power. If they could, it would free them up to let others grow and prosper. That's the key when you have self-love and self-awareness: It's hard to hurt others. You see, we are all energetically connected. The harm you cause others reverberates back to you and affects you in many ways.

To put what has been happening into the simplest terms: It is only real because you think it is real; if you think it is not real, it is unreal. Act accordingly; think and feel your way into the truth of who you know yourself to be. Do not allow yourself to be defined by others. If marginalization is obvious within the culture you are associated with, make decisions to oppose it or leave for a better situation in a new environment. Remember to leave the previous bias where you saw it. Do not bring the hurt into the new environment.

We may consider it difficult to release our old beliefs because we fear losing the feeling of solid, familiar ground. We tell ourselves it happened, and *I will be vigilant to fight it if I see it again*. With that thought, we look for any hint that it might be happening again. To fully examine your thinking, employ debate rules; study the subject from a position you have not considered.

Identify areas where your solid-ground belief might not be the truth.

Could your belief be preventing you from freely living as your authentic self?

A yes to either question suggests examination is a viable option. Still your thoughts and allow time and quiet space to process. Decide if these old triggers are your current feelings or thoughts.

If it is upsetting, ask yourself:

- *What am I resisting?*
- *What can I learn from this?*

Don't ask anyone what they think until you have first thought it through for yourself.

I weep when I see people on television who are doing what they are meant to do and are making a great difference in this world. For the longest time, I could not understand why I would cry at something so wonderful. It dawned on me that I was weeping because people are just people. The colorism, the marginalization, the sexualization—none of those are real because they are constructs, created to hold people in a certain place. My tears are an understanding that the people who are living their lives to their fullest, beyond their fears and other people's rhetoric, are real heroes.

We can lay down for ourselves any belief that racism, marginalization, and oppression are real roadblocks. You can lay down notions that do not uplift you. Embrace the concept that you can and will no longer believe in that bogus power.

I know many people who will say: *How dare you! How could you say racism does not exist?* Colorism does exist in an oppressor's contrived manipulation; however, I'm taking responsibility for my thinking to say: *It no longer exists in my mind as a belief that can hold me back*. The notion of it not being acceptable is my freedom walk mentally and energetically.

When you are true to yourself, there is no need to be anyone else. Do the best you know how and live with that joy! Be who you came here to be and trust you are more than enough. It doesn't matter what our tribe says, what a government says, what corporate heads say because what matters is what you as an individual came here to do while your efforts contribute to making the world a better place.

As you meditate on the craving to do what Spirit has placed in your heart, you rouse yourself from longing to remain on the seemingly easy road. By *the easy road*, I mean accepting what others say and doing what is asked of you even while you are feeling dissatisfied. You gather energy as you shift awareness to the path ahead.

I'm not talking about the challenge of going along; rather, the yearning to step onto the new path, away from routine, and into the exceptional personal dares. Thrust yourself on the first step and let your heart become infused with desire to recognize the reality of your own power. Watch how new opportunities and conversations make a difference in your world when you allow yourself to be the person you were born to be.

Why would an Omnipotent Energy create you and then punish you for being what was created? Does that make sense to you? When you are so exhausted you want to run away, will you then be able to stop the habitual pattern that is binding you?

The ego wants to show others what it senses the world wants to see, who you wish you were, as if who you really are isn't good enough. Who you are is enough! The people who implied otherwise didn't know any better than to tease, berate, or shame you. And make no mistake; I'm not talking about your angry-self. I'm not talking about your sensitive side that hides behind snark or humor. I am referring to your loving and nonfearful self you came here to be. That is your greatness.

Exercise: Define Yourself

Take action to free your mind from ideas that hold you hostage, whether you adopted them when you were a child or adult. You may want to journal or record your thoughts about your decision and your thoughts as you go through each step. Thinking differently and releasing burdens become reality when we consciously and regularly practice. Rather than judge ourselves harshly when we fall short, we restart—again and again when necessary. We are training our brain to think in a new way, and that takes practice and time. Critical judgments do not forward positive and powerful thinking.

Step1: Decide to release your burdensome thinking of *I'm not good enough* or *I cannot change*. You know you feel as though you're not good enough if your current thoughts leave you feeling heavy, invisible to yourself, unhappy, or unable to see yourself with the same kindness you extend to others. Believing you cannot change is an internal choice, that you have the ability to change. Write or record reasons you find it important to change.

Step 2: Explore your burdens by analyzing the possibility your information has been wrong.

How would you see yourself if you lifted the veil of self-disregard and agreed to see and share the best within you? Describe how that could feel. How would you live differently as you interact with others? How would you talk about yourself differently?

Step 3: Identify steps to return to your joyful place. How can you encourage yourself when you feel out of sorts?

Step 4: Thinking differently and releasing burdens can be a freeing reality. Document how you will give yourself grace and compliments every day for each tiny improvement. List what you will say to yourself. Say it to yourself at regular intervals throughout the day and before you close your eyes to sleep.

Step 5: Acknowledge you did not perish because you thought well of yourself. Notice the kind things you do for yourself. Remind yourself you are devoting yourself to increase your well-being.

Step 6: Promote kindness in your heart—kindness toward yourself first, then your home and family, outward to your friends, and then your community. If you feel like you don't know how to do that, just ask yourself: *What I would say to a stranger?* Or *What would I want a stranger to say to me?* And then, say it to yourself.

Step 7: Give yourself permission to love yourself. It all starts within you. No one is responsible for making you feel better or worse about yourself. Once you grow up, as an adult, you take responsibility for your well-being. You will run into people—some may even be friends of yours—who will blame everybody else for their own unhappiness or not feeling included. You can be an example to them, but you cannot change their way of looking at themselves. That is their responsibility.

I want you to remember this: Extend to yourself the kindness you want to see from others. You accept that responsibility for and to yourself. No one else can make you feel better about you. You'll most likely find that those who do *make you* feel better fail you at some point; feeling good about yourself is an inside job.

If you're in love with somebody, you may say they make you feel good; however, it's not their responsibility to constantly try to make you feel better. It is your own responsibility. When you take that responsibility seriously, you can train yourself to be kinder to yourself. You set yourself up for life that is a joy to live. I'm not saying you won't have ups and downs. That's part of being human. It's often the way we learn.

I told the Universe: *I'm a smart person, and I no longer choose to learn through painful experience.* I had a great long run, until I didn't. It was my responsibility to journey with myself, to refocus and begin again. In this space, I found the ability to see through what was happening in front of me, what people were going through. I could sense their pain and, therefore, not take personally what they said or how they acted.

If you must think of yourself as a newborn baby learning how to walk again, that's fine. We don't yell at a baby for falling. We understand they fall, and they must get back up. You may forget that you're on your journey to thinking and feeling better about yourself. That's when you fall, and that's when you pick yourself back up. There is no need for judgment of that baby when they fall; it's just what happens. There's no judgment needed of yourself if you fall off the path to self-love. Shake it off and start again. You continue this for the rest of your life. It's better than spending the day resting on old thought processes that keep you down energetically.

Mind Shift: Positive Reinforcement

Create a list of positive quotes or affirmations. You can grab a book or google a list of positive quotes or better yet: create a list of your own. I use a mala and I repeat the quote 108 times. I can see and feel evidence of the energetic shift within me. With practice, you can create a natural shift of an experience as quickly as your intention is set. Persist to incorporate the energetic tone within your mind and your body. Repeat as needed.

Your Divine Purpose

Your purpose is not an unsolvable mystery. It is what you are called to do. Others wonder how you do it so effortlessly when they can't grasp it. They have different abilities to share with the world. Your purpose is your expression. You come alive when you do it. It need not be perceived by the world as grandiose. You could be doing it with your neighbors, your coworkers or with an elder or younger person. Your uniqueness makes the interaction special.

If someone says, "Who do you think you are?" you now have some idea that you have personal power and how to use it in your everyday life, should you change your thoughts to design the life you desire. Do not waste your time focusing your thoughts on what other people should or should not do or say; rather, focus your energy and think on what you can do to be who you were meant to be and accomplish the activities that suit your life's pursuits. The center of our being has no conflict, it is our intimate connection with the Creation of our own design.

Chapter Four

Trust Versus Fear

The beauty of trust is multifaceted, enhancing all aspects of our lives. Trusting something greater than our mortal self acknowledges what I call a *Source Force Energy* that we can tap into at any time. We are so much more than our bodies. We humans are also spiritual beings, no matter our individual beliefs. Our spiritual self is built from within, as it is the energy we are born with that leaves us when we die. Trusting ourselves and our inner energy source creates a greater sense of confidence. We feel empowered to take chances to fulfill and further our desires and purpose. When you have faith in yourself, you become more comfortable in your authenticity and decision making. Each time you share your authentic self, you create within yourself a greater sense of well-being and deeper connection with the people destined to be in your life.

Mind Shift: The Design Power of "If"

A good exercise toward trusting yourself is based on understanding the word *if* as a powerful conjunction in determining or stating your desires. This practice ignites your own permission to seek and obtain your greatest dream life.

Describe what your desire could look like in your everyday life.

Put the word *if* in a statement ahead of your desire. When you do, you open brain pathways to support the possibility of that very thing happening. You are signaling to your unconscious you are open to allowing that to happen in your life.

For example:

If I were the owner of a small business that helped people to grow the most beautiful flowers . . .

List the ways your life would vary—as many ways as your imagination has to offer.

Write how you would feel trusting your dream coming true.

What emotions and thoughts would you carry within yourself?

How would accepting this dream bring you closer to being your more authentic self?

Expand your imagination. Would you be a storyteller to young children in libraries? Would you honor your voice and record voiceovers? Can you imagine yourself helping people build up more wealth by sharing techniques on how to grow their finances? Would you share gardening techniques to help people create more beauty in their surroundings?

Perhaps you can imagine performing or speaking onstage in front of an audience. The possibilities are endless when you decide to trust pursuing your dream and sharing it with all who can be touched by what you have to share.

Maybe your dream seems too lofty, but your heart sings at the idea, your palms sweat a little, or unexpected tears appear at the possibility. These are all signs you are receiving a message from within.

You want to sing? Start sharing your voice in small ways: sing to yourself and to your family, create a social media account and sing songs to inspire other people, join a choir, find a voice coach. You decide to keep moving forward, inch by inch, until momentum builds. Watch how the little steps lead to your bigger adventures. You learn a lot about yourself when you pay attention while going slowly. By the time your biggest dreams arrive, you are better prepared mentally and emotionally to accept your good fortune and its ability to help others. Taking these small steps over time teaches you to trust yourself. You learn through lived experience to embody this new circumstance and own it—to embrace it as who you are and what you do.

An added benefit of developing trust is that you release your dependency on following exclusively the directions of others. Trusting yourself switches on an inner flashlight that shines on your desire to live and love yourself and others as you choose. As you accept responsibility and your right to shift into your own power, the path no longer eludes you. Notice the quality of the thinking that supports you to replace disappointment with joyful expression. This is how you build trust within yourself, incrementally at first and bountifully through practice.

As your acceptance of your internal confidence grows, sadness shifts to joy. You seek awareness and the freedom to divine and define your rewarding life. You are required to relinquish your tight hold to control how you appear to others. Open your mind and heart to trust the Universe's desire-energy to be your coconspirator in creating your very best life.

I've met people who could not acknowledge or trust their feelings. Others had a difficult time identifying positive feelings with their successes. I've heard them dismiss the good they have done with statements like: *It wasn't anything important*, or *It only took me a few minutes, no big deal*. When others raved about the great work, these people could not accept the compliment. They could not admit how helpful they had been and were unable to give themselves credit.

Their perception, informed by their self-talk, couldn't make space for their unique brilliance. Established patterns of interaction had blurred their ability to trust a positive sense of self. They were still holding onto words from people who didn't think them capable of doing great work, and it continued to haunt them for decades.

Many of these people had teachers who had labeled them inaccurately because of the teacher's preconceived notions about the student's background, family origin, test scores, or race.

Teachers: If you have forgotten how much power you have when speaking to a child, just listen to adults and watch them beam when asked about their favorite teachers. Kindness is so critical to a child's development. Whether a child is encouraged and recognized by their teacher is vital to how they feel, how their days evolve, and how their long-term self-talk is affected.

I hope teachers will keep ever present in their hearts how influential their role is to the betterment of our world, helping to produce socially and emotionally stronger graduates. I know friends and clients both who can still quote what a teacher said to them that ripped their self-confidence. We can all recall the teachers who poured the positivity into our development that still brings a smile to our faces.

Which teacher will you be for any child you interact with?

Facades of Fear

Trusting your highest, best-self energy is a concept that can evoke fear in the hearts of people who do not want to be thought of as arrogant. *Who am I to fulfill this desire?* Before embarking on the path of empowerment, it may be difficult to trust that upsetting the familiar dynamics will be a good thing. You may imagine fears of losing love, losing income, or ruining your perceived standing in the community.

Are you wondering what is your best and highest self and whether it's worth compromising the life you are living?

Your highest, best self is your soul's goal. It is your joy-centered, integrity-filled, playful, thoughtful, and loving self. It accepts others and yourself without a need to judge mistakes, so that you may learn from them. It extends grace in order to receive grace when you or I make a mistake as we climb toward our best self. Your highest, best self is the understanding you might need help to be able to live your best life and your highest calling.

When we are conditioned to think less of ourselves and our abilities, we follow the rules, trundling along like good toddlers in grown bodies. We trust others' opinions of us and our situations. This is what creates the weight of fear we live under, as if it is scheduled on our mental calendar daily.

This program has been with you so long, it is written in your mind with indelible ink. I'm speaking of the fear that is internal—not the external forces in the world that we fear, such as war, poverty, and impending violence. There are internal fears, such as not speaking up, not clearly seeing our own gifts, and not trusting we have a purpose. Giving our power to others renders us powerless to hearing our own voice's power and needs.

People who convince themselves they need love but don't know how to get it turn to blame and shame. They create opportunities for other people to suffer as much as they are suffering. We may see their cruel behavior as a cry for help. When we witness the worst deeds from human hands daily on our local news, most of us do not understand them as extreme cries for help. Have empathy for those who commit those acts because many more people than we can imagine are living with smoldering hostility toward themselves and others while hiding it behind a pretend smile.

I know firsthand the brutal blows life can deal to us from childhood through to adulthood. I also know if we hold tightly to the things that happened to us, we lose perspective and the ability to enjoy and recreate the good things. We block loving experiences from happening in our lives.

It is important to understand the fears that cause you to hide your true self:

- What fear-based limits are you placing upon yourself?
- How are your fears keeping you or your life small?
- What energy level do you want regularly in your life?

Higher and lower vibrational energy attracts itself. No energy is wasted. Choose wisely what energy you want to emit and receive. Energy travels with wings on our thoughts. If you do not like what you're experiencing, change what are you are saying to yourself. Uplift your energy with positive thoughts that lead to emotions aligned with your positive thinking. Remember to watch and acknowledge the change.

If it helps, think of your thoughts as prayers. You are thinking a thought, and it resides on your personal energy like wings. If your thoughts are low and fear-based, your wings are too weak to lift you up. Every time you rehearse your repetitive low-energy thoughts, restate them based on the positive things you want and visualize your thoughts as wings lifting you as high as you are willing to believe in any situation.

Love edges out fear. Love is the superpower, and fear is merely the ego, trying to heighten its power by saturating you with low thoughts of negativity and unworthiness. Ego becomes the saboteur, obstructing what is good and promoting thoughts that hamper positive progress and hurt relationships. You give it power when you align its energy to your thoughts and internal storytelling. Fear-thinking assumes there is something to fear around each corner, on every block, and believes the violence reported on the evening news is happening outside your door, when in fact, there isn't a murder, rape, or theft every day on your block. You are consistently creating low, angst-ridden energy.

After the pandemic, I talked to several people who were afraid of getting in their car or sitting inside the car because the twenty-four-hour news cycle said people's cars were being carjacked at alarming rates. I know people who have been carjacked. I had a decision to make. I chose to change the way I thought about entering my car, and to change the energy I was emitting into the world. Friends and I made a pack to stop giving our energetic power to fear-thoughts of getting in and out of our vehicles. We did not want to attract energetically what we didn't want in the ethers.

We asked: *What energy vibration do we want?* In my case, it was a safety watch—watch my thoughts and disavow the ones that were paralyzing me. I replaced thoughts of fear with thoughts of attracting positivity.

Mind Shift: Shifting Energy

You can shift Energy by repeating powerful thoughts. I use either a mala or rosary beads or hold a small smooth stone in my hand when I know exactly what I need to say to shift my energy. When I don't have a mantra, I use a notebook to journal how I am feeling, using descriptive words to convey my current thoughts and how they make me feel in that moment.

This creates awareness and acknowledges what is currently running havoc in my mind.

Create or find a mantra to be repeated that will lift your awareness out of where you are currently. If you can't think of anything to write or a mantra to help move yourself, ask:

What do I want to feel instead of this?

Create a positive statement based on what you want to think and feel.

Begin saying the mantra and breathing intentionally. Notice the changes you go through without judging. I have started out sad, ready to cry, letting tears fall, waiting for what is next. And typically, I feel a centered energy coming over me.

Did I just smile as I got halfway through the beads?

What speed am I saying this at? How does it feel right? Faster, quieter, out loud and slower?

When I finish at 108 beads, my mood is completely shifted. It is in this moment I can set a positive intention for the rest of my day. If I slip backward toward a lower energy vibration, I have but to recall the mantra and begin repeating it. No one need know. I am going to my happier place to be better internally and vibrating higher as I interact with people I encounter. The exercise opens feelings of great peace. I can see and feel evidence of the energetic shift within me.

Don't fret if you start out just saying words with no feelings involved. With repetition, you will internalize the meaning and higher energy of the words. At first, the shift into peaceful feelings can take nearly the entire strand. As you practice, you can shift and acknowledge the natural loving smile that appears more quickly. Keep going to set the vibrational energy tone within your mind and body.

When I am talking about fear, I'm not referring to the fear of facing someone who is actively physically or psychologically violent toward you. I'm talking about the fear we adopt to make ourselves smaller. We watch the violence in the world, and we think it keeps us abreast of what is happening around us. We think the perpetrator is outside the door, and if a perpetrator has never been outside your door, you are still fearful. That form of thinking is hurting you. I am describing the fear that has energy that feeds us messages, that believes doomsday is a permanent fixture in your thinking patterns and, therefore, your life. I'm talking about compounded fear that builds up and distorts your vision of life and people you don't even know. Your connections and interactions with others get smaller.

Mind and Heart Are Personal

Think of the letter Y as your mind-heart connection. The base of the Y is the vertical we stand on. The opening at the top is your heart on the left and your thoughts on the right. Their connection is the middle opening—vast and unlimited space that reaches toward the sky. You have a choice. You can open to unlimited goodness if your energy is high or unlimited despair if your energy is habitually low. When the heart and mind are united, your heart can lead, and your mind can follow. As we allow our heart to lead, our goal is unity with our self. Adult self-love is ignited with the love that brought us into the world at birth.

When we allow our mind alone to lead, we go after vain undertakings. Living by our mind from childhood forward is a sure path to allowing that love to shrivel and lie dormant as we take on the rules and regulations of the outer world. That outer world thinking begins at our first home. In our early youth, our whole world is our family/guardian structure and rules. That's where we pick up our dysfunction clues we later apply in the world while trying to survive. What we experience in the home becomes the lens through which we see and judge (think thoughts about), even though we are outside the view of our family structure. It's a very insularly created world because it's all we knew at the time.

When we are sent off to school, we meet teachers, coaches, principals, and administrators who also have expectations. Let us not forget, all those other children in the classroom, school hallway, cafeteria, and playground bring their nuclear beliefs, and the clashing of ideas about behavior ensues. There are friendships to be made, there are hurts to be inflicted and felt, there are misunderstandings. These add building blocks to how we interpret the world when we begin to merely exist rather than show up as our full self.

When reality feels like other people telling you how you should live your life, after a while their suggestions feel like demands that put limits on your authentic being. If you allow that reality to persist, you slowly allow them to shift who you are, how you are, and where you go. It is tiring to live in a reality that does not support your most natural self. It is a life of smiling on the outside while your insides are hurting, searching for relief, and crying silently: *Is this all there is to my life?* It's a sure indication that if you fear your own truth enough to allow others to take over, you extinguish who you are meant to be. Each phase of your life feels like another layer of reality that closes the top of your Y.

You know your Y is closing in on you when you lose yourself and any trust related to your own importance. We take this human experience with all the hurts and pains as it becomes a compounded personal tragedy. Feeling lost to your true self is a wakeup siren, screaming something is off-base and needs attention, such as a new way of thinking.

Sometimes I must back away from everything and everyone to get clear about feelings and happenings. I don't allow myself to back away for too long because self-absorption can lie to me and strongly encourage me to keep my distance and not to trust anyone or let anyone in because the interaction won't be helpful.

When we are struggling in fear, it is so real. But it's not, because the truth of the matter is we can perceive fear as a wakeup call, telling us to examine closely what is happening. It tells us we can make a better choice. Because what is real is trusting the truth of our individual being and the right of others to choose what is right for them.

How to live in a triggering world?

How to accept yourself when your community condones your way of being?

Recognize that when our thoughts attack other people, we are creating energy within us that destroys and lowers our own well-being; thereby, we suffer. When I worry, I must look for evidence to support myself feeling out of sorts. If I mistrust people around me when they are showing their human tragic selves, I hurt because the energy triggers greater mistrust I have within myself. I look for evidence to support the distrust by telling myself stories to prove my thoughts are true. Now I have made myself feel all-out miserable. I am obsessing.

When feeling triggered, you need to have ready solutions, such as reading over your foundational beliefs or repeating one of the affirmations listed below. And, as always, you can create your own supportive affirmations for uplifting change.

Here are examples of positive affirmations:

- *I am not your opinion of me.*
- *I have the right to feel my feelings.*
- *I have the capability of feeling my feelings and letting them go when they no longer serve me.*
- *My feelings signal when to stay in the moment and when it's time to change course.*
- *My feelings are a barometer in my life.*

- *I am abundant. My mind and heart share my abundance with the world.*
- *My feelings are related to my thoughts.*
- *I am capable of changing my thoughts and my feelings.*
- *Sitting with my feelings can reveal new ways of thinking.*

Choosing our right to be our authentic selves sets up our individuality. How we are different matters only insofar as how we use our differences to help support each other. We are born different. We embrace our uniqueness, rather than try to conform to other people's ideas of what we should be. It's time to get comfortable with our uniqueness while accepting other people's uniqueness.

You may be grateful to get home and close the door on the outside world. Or, you may keep yourself always on the go, always moving, so you do not have time to think about what is so awful about the way life has unfolded. It's time to trust that you can handle a variety of situations. I recall a man I worked with telling me he could not be home without the television or music being turned on. I asked why and he said, "because I can't stand being alone with my own thoughts."

Imagine how much fear there must be, to not want to be still or quiet with yourself; the one person you are with day in and day out.

If you are a giver to others and aren't feeling good about it, part of the answer is *stop*. Fill yourself back up. Give kindness to yourself. Give attention to yourself. Ground yourself back to giving from your overflow and not for a return of love or money or power over the other person. If your destiny is power, use it to help yourself and others. If you crave power to fill a void, you may get power, but it won't fulfill the darkest recesses of your mind, heart, or body.

We get so accustomed to the limitations our mental chains produce that we accept them as our norm. Without examination, we live within limits that are self-proclaimed, and we lie to ourselves, saying: *This is just the way it is.* We attract people who assist in keeping us in chains.

I'm here to say it doesn't have to be that way. Chains can be rattled. Unchained and unhinged, those chains can be tossed aside. You must be stronger than the conceptual chain that you attached to your daily living. I use my mind and heart to serve a God that is Ultimate Love.

To serve love is to be love. It is to live in honesty; it is me, trusting love. It is me, being nonjudgmental and nonresistant to what is happening. When we see with love, a wounded person can appear in our lives, and we don't have to take on a fear of what they might do or say. We can consciously choose not to focus on their exhibited wounds but rather focus on heart-to-heart connections because we are all connected by the energy of love. Imagine if we all turned up love just one notch, how we could be free to be, rather than needing to show our sickest self through heinous acts of distraction and destruction. Spiritual energy can help tame the wayward mind, while physical energy cannot. Love is creation of connection without judgment or resistance.

You never know how your kindness and authentic self can impact another person. While visiting with family in the south, I was taking my daily walk as a man was leaving his house to get into his car. As most southerners do, we greeted each other with mutual good mornings, and I added, "How are you today?"

His response has stayed with me. He said, "Today is my best day."

This was an early morning walk, so the day had just started, but he declared his intention and shared it with me, a stranger to him in the normal sense of the word, but a fellow human being in a loving space. I don't know his name, but I've been using what he said as one of my go-to intentions. I am forever thankful to him for sharing his great attitude with me. That is my best example of how to positively impact the start of your day and others' days as well.

Mind Shift: Morning Thoughts

Pay attention to your early morning thoughts. The first thoughts that run through your mind are critical.

When I would wake up after not having had enough sleep, my thoughts could be fearful and dark and create an ominous dread on the day. I am aware enough now to ease my thoughts to allow myself to go into meditation. Once my mind is centered, I declare my true intention for the day.

Start the morning with positive thoughts. Allow Creation Energy to go before you throughout the day. Watch how uplifted you feel.

I am checking in with the elevated internal flow of energy. I feel a creative flow in my legs, and it tells my brain it's time to create. I am grateful my center has returned. No judgment nor fear of other people, family, politicians, neighbors, and strangers on the street. To critique them is to critique myself. And it doesn't improve my internal peace levels.

There is no need to compare your life situations to others. Being grateful that your life is better than someone else's is not love. It is not gratitude-worthy because we are all connected energetically. We are all one.

Cultural Fits and Misfits

The days of groupthink or cultural norms needing to be absolute are waning. Those rules are energetically weighing people down. People are tiring of trying to fit into molds that don't fit them. The lesson is: Sharing our differences creates a stronger experience for all. When we bond with people, it often develops over our similarities. As we get to know each other better, we see our differences more clearly. The connection becomes more comfortable when we share all sides of ourselves with each other. Differences don't make one person right and another wrong. They just make us different.

When people feel they have the right to control you and your life, they are trusting themselves to see you as they would have you be, which challenges your ability to trust yourself to handle what life presents. As I put the period to that sentence, I could hear people saying, "You're darn right—because life is hard, and I'm trying to help me and my family to keep things on a straight path in a crazy world!"

That kind of controlling help doesn't help us avoid what life presents. It does not teach our children how to cope and get back up after adversity. It creates in us a closed heart that struggles to beat at its natural rhythm. The old ways need to be laid down, that we may resurrect resilience. And I know that the controllers fear that there will be anarchy, and their world as they know it will combust. I offer another consideration. My counter is this: Haven't we lived long enough with the chaos that says we must carry on the way we have for generations? Doesn't it feel like the world is combusting around us with the old ways of handling things? The way of *be quiet—we don't discuss those types of things!* is crumbling. Or *shut down the way you are feeling, you will grow out of it*, but you now know you won't. The old paradigm of expecting to hide your true self and still be happy is not working. It is not possible because it is not rooted in truth and personal responsibility.

Fear in the modern work world is more consistent in overworked, overwrought, and anxiety-driven work environments. If you can boast about working late into the night or over the weekend and not taking all your vacation time, then you are not protecting yourself from the oppression of an insecure management culture. One client would hold her body tightly to be prepared for the next unrealistic request in an already tightly filled to do list. Fear, remember, shuts us down.

Your creativity suffers and you forget things as simple as words or appointments. You wonder what is going on, and at times, you just can't put your finger on it. Dealing in a stressful, profit-led environment has you on a struggle bus.

All of the unexamined years of expectations pile up and beg us at some point to question by whose standard are we living our life today? If the answer isn't your own, you are doing yourself a disservice. There will be ideas and beliefs that fit cultural norms, and some don't fit for your authentic self. If you have a need to keep secrets or hide your preferences for fear of how others will accept you, you are granting others more power in your life than you grant yourself. Giving away your one life puts your well-being at risk.

I'm proposing it is time for a new way of creating the life you want with less fear and more trust of yourself and those around you—a life with meaning and purpose, joy, genuine laughter, and peace of mind. If your mind is scattered, find what you love to do and scatter that loving gesture in the world. Bring your focus to what you want. Every thought you don't want, tell it to fly away. That allows you to bring in the thoughts of what you do want.

Set your intention as soon as you wake up for the kind of days and nights you want. That way you are practiced, so when your murky mind tries to go amok, you can say definitively "No, no."

Exercise: Morning Intentions

Here's an exercise to help you set the tone for the intention you do want to create.

Each morning, set the intention for the day ahead. Repeat the intention numerous times as you are dressing for the day. For example, if I wake up with a murky mind, I don't try to figure out why anymore. I say, "No thank you. My intention for today is a gold mine, so I don't and won't entertain that thankless thought anymore."

♡

Direct your thoughts away from what you don't want to thoughts of what you do want to create. More love and open honesty are better for relationships and better for a more fulfilling life. The energy you invest in living happily with others is energy well spent. It gives you memories of the treasured times you've created and can reflect on when those people have left this Earth.

There is a positive voice I hear in moments of struggle that says: *There is a purpose for this.* That gives me the space to reflect, to seek deeper understanding within myself. I listen for words throughout the day to hear the message that is trying to get through. One morning I was feeling insecure about relationships in my life. I wasn't feeling good about myself because I wasn't showing up as me. I was showing up totally focused externally, imagining what I could do to make these relationships better and forfeiting my own desires and power. That morning, I set two intentions for the day. First, to be kind to myself; and second, to not give in to self-limiting, insecure thoughts.

Giving away your power is not attractive to you or the other person. Once I had set my intentions, I could pay attention to what I saw and heard. For example, I heard on television and in church the song "Amazing Grace," a sign I needed to give myself some grace. Secondly, two friends spoke to me in meaningful ways. Unprompted, they both shared how they felt about me in their lives. One said, "You have influenced me in ways you cannot imagine. Please continue to allow your light to shine." The second person said, "Your authentic living helped to shape our change in our dysfunctional workplace."

I had no idea people felt that way. The second person continued to say, "Are you kidding? People were often falling into your office or following you around to just share and hear your encouragement." Those comments were reinforcement to live in my authentic authority, to shine my light brightly and live in that light.

You also possess authentic authority that the world needs to experience.

Years ago, I became ready and open to learn what the Universe would have me learn. I voiced an intention that I was ready to embrace the miracles the Universe offers. I vowed to release thoughts I had held on to that hurt me.

You can make the choice by reflecting on trust or lack of trust as well. Ask yourself:

- *How can I change my way of thinking so that I am free from believing people cannot be trusted?*
- *How do I return to trusting when I have been disappointed?*
- *How do I break free from the thoughts I have in a healthy way for me and for my relationships?*

I had to be willing to change my perception. I reminded myself to stay in the present moment and embrace when I was being treated well—to notice when I trusted people, I could see the innocence in the other person, for judging them forces me to judge myself. It's a way to typically disregard unworthy thoughts and feelings. A spotlight on the pesky ego showed me it tries to engage with me when it thinks my energy is low. Changing my perception changed my energy to a higher awareness that made me less susceptible to being dragged down by ego.

I worked with clients for whom mid-year and annual review times in their jobs were stressful. Being evaluated was fraught with anxiety. They had worked so hard for so long, and the feedback was rarely focused on what they did well. Even when the majority of the review was excellent, all they could focus on were the one or two less-than-favorable responses. It would eat at them in a deeply personal way. Taming the mind to focus on what is good and excellent and giving it greater weight than the minor criticisms requires discipline and a shift in thinking.

The answers are within you. You must be willing to sit with the fear and listen for your Divine Intuition. Sit with fear, anger, disappointment, and discontent until you gather a peace that allows you to think clear and kind thoughts for yourself and to see the reviewer's human frailties. Understand where they are coming from and what caused them to write what they did. Ask clarifying questions after you have calmed down. Negotiate a revision if you have counterpoints to be considered.

We are not here to be perfect. We are here to learn and grow.

Chapter Five

Q

Leave Fear: Embrace
Freedom Living

Habitual fear-thoughts are not true. Again, I am not referring to actual incidents facing you in the present moment that may be violent toward your spirit or body. We recall from Chapter Two that fear can be a benefit; it can incent us to make a change, move forward, or stand in the space of harm to protect ourselves. In this chapter, we talk about the habitual fear-based thought that hinders movement toward what you want to do and how you interact in this world. Habitual hindering thoughts range from *Life is hard* to *I have no energy to work out, engage with others, or care about anything.*

By now you have likely identified some of your habitual hindering thoughts. And if you have not, listen to your self-talk. Be clear and aware of how you talk to yourself before you answer this question:

Am I willing to stay discontented and disillusioned because that's the way it's been for so long?

When we stay too long in discontentment and delusion, we feel like we have lost sight of ourselves. You don't know who you are or what you want, couldn't name your desire if anyone asked you to—you're not even sure how to define what your purpose is and not certain why this pattern of living is repeating itself. This is your: *Hey me, where have you been?* moment. I have been there several times and realized I might find myself there again as life circumstances move and shift, as the people around me shift and change.

When I feel like I'm losing my sense of self in any relationship—friends, love interests, coworkers, family, bosses, board seats—it is likely because of what I saw and heard in my initial address that has not been examined or in the habits I built to protect myself. My goal is to linger no longer in thoughts such as: *This is unfair* and *Why is this happening to me?*

To alleviate a long road to return to myself, I review the following questions:

- *What part of what is happening is my responsibility?*
- *What responsibility, if any, belongs to the other person?*
- *Where did I learn this way of being?*
- *What circumstances could my young-person brain have misconstrued?*
- *Is this what I want to continue to repeat?*
- *What is so threatening to me about this trigger?*
- *Is what I perceive of this situation really true?*

These questions are my search for the real Deborah answers. You are welcome to start your own inner dialogue with the questions above when you're feeling off-center or emotionally lost. You are certainly free to design your own deep-dive-into-freedom questions. The question *Is it true?* is last, following your conscious gathering of facts and thoughts to make a new assessment.

Self-examination liberates us to make new and improved alignment within ourselves. It allows us to be unequivocally who we want to be, such as our best and authentic self. How we garnered love and learned to negotiate love as children doesn't have to apply in the world outside our family or in adulthood inside our family. Others come with their inherited-by-association beliefs that may assert we are wrong because it's not what they saw early on in their lives.

Take the time to understand what serves you best, to remain present with those you interact with, and attract the people you desire in your life. Relationships may teach you new perspectives that empower you more. Those who try to dim your light to meet their requirements for relationship or who expect you to live under their light are trying to snuff out your brightness. The burden of living snuffed out is hard because denying your best self is stifling, and ultimately, we own the damaging neglect. The reason you are here is not too be stifled. You are here to be your best and brightest self.

We were born with authenticity that doesn't question our self-worth or whether we are good enough. Let's be clear: living freely does not exclude us from hard days; it does not magically eliminate challenges; instead, it allows us to journey into our own way of evaluating and growing. We get to discover, live, and appreciate our way of being as we deem appropriate in any situation. Daily awareness allows us to acknowledge ourselves whenever we are feeling emotional. We can say, "I am afraid" or "I'm feeling fearful" when we are authentic, before we decide where to leave our feelings—whether that's on a steppingstone or deeper inside our thinking. When we go inside, we analyze the fear by asking ourselves a probing question:

Does this feeling represent anything from my past?

Digging into your past for understanding allows you to identify and clear past misbeliefs down to the root of your authentic story. That clearing firmly plants you on your authentic foundation to support your desire toward freedom living. Beware of the stories based on individual viewpoints you heard when you were growing up. Take the good and decide to discard the weight you have put into the not-so-pleasant parts of the stories you were told. Identify the good aspects of who you are that came out of the unpleasant memories. Be proud of what you have discovered.

However, if those fear-thoughts persist in your mind, you have a recourse: you decide to change your mind, and you decide to what degree you accept the notion of the change.

The Universe wants us to be happy, to be content, and to feel safe because we are the design of the Highest Energy, and that energy is part of our very being. That is personal freedom. Concentrate on the concept of what life would be like—the freedom possibilities it could open up—if you had little-to-no fear or distrust of people in general, including those you do not know personally. We can understand at the deepest level *love* is our salvation.

Here are a couple of questions for you:

- Are you willing to see things differently for a more inspired life?
- Is it time to shine a new and brighter light to eradicate unfounded chronic fear, inadequate self-judgment, false tales, and worries about limitation?

It's decision time, and only you can make the decision that leads to the fortitude and conviction needed to initiate your personal change. It is faith, not fear, that brings us to our desires. Understand and trust that your thoughts can be managed without apprehension. Changing your thoughts can change your life for the better to live freely as you were meant to live. Moving your thinking can illuminate your possibilities, and that can actualize your dreams. Worry disconnects you from the flow of abundance.

Bringing our humanness closer in line with our holiness is our purest plan: to be love and share love. Living in that space evokes freedom. Our humanness is good, but we have been conditioned to not see it clearly. The perceptions in our minds don't allow us to think highly of ourselves. We believe the bad things whispered and sometimes shouted to us, and they obscure and blind us so thoroughly that we ignore the good that is inherent in being our human self.

We put on blinders to the surrounding good. It is as if we are laser-focused on a mental lookout, confirming something terrible is always on the way. This is not a pleasant way to live. There is a powerful way to reverse your framework. Haven't you lived long enough powering into what you do not want? We are born out of creation, and therefore, we are creators. You get to decide to create good or evil and love or self-loathing. You choose what produces your highest energy level.

Freedom in Forgiveness

Forgiveness liberates you from feeling miserable within your mind and body. Our thoughts of holding on to what someone did or said sprinkles in us intermittent melancholy. It isolates us from another view of what we perceive has been done to us. Forgiveness is also our freedom from continuing to feel the pangs of internal discomfort.

When the thought of what *that person* said or did enters your mind, you have the ability to cancel that thought. Do it quickly to avoid going down the rabbit hole. If you go down the deep hole, time suspends; it can be minutes to hours later, and you are still feeling the effects of harboring ill will toward someone you likely do not see regularly.

You get to decide how you want to feel about that old hurt: let it go, or continually entertain thoughts about the infraction. Give yourself permission to feel sad, and create suffering; or give yourself permission to release the perception, and move past suffering to residual peace and personal freedom.

It is your choice. Choose wisely.

Forgiving someone else opens space to forgive yourself. None of us is perfect. We may not have done as dastardly a deed as we put on our offender, but if we can't forgive someone else, then we cannot expect someone to forgive us, and that makes it even harder to forgive ourselves.

We are all seeking connection. You have no idea the suffering your offender may have experienced before they hurt you and then after they hurt you. Forgive their frailties and see beyond the deed to their heart. Take your focus off hurt and trying to change them. This will give you freedom to be fully present in the present moment.

A coaching client and I had numerous heart-to-heart conversations about his mother, who is not aging as gracefully as he would hope to see in his parent in her golden years. He has been anxious and seeking peace for most of his life. After many hours of discussion and self-examination, he felt inspired to be able to see the childlike spirit in his mother.

He found he could feel peace as he removed judgment and hurt from his thinking about her. She has been fighting to be seen as an upstanding person outwardly. Yet, behind that facade was a frightened person who struck out at her family members, like a soap opera diva, saying whatever needs to be said in the moment to protect her standing in her mind.

He tells me he can see clearly now that "none of what she did was meant to hurt me." It was meant to protect her sense of self. His sense of anger and sadness are gone. He accepts her and does not judge her for the wounding outbursts. Nor will he any longer take personally what she says. That is his new thinking that led to his forgiveness, nonjudgment, and a greater sense of freedom to be present with his parent.

Being angry with elderly parents energetically hurts them and us. As adults, we do not require their validation. So, recognize it may be awful for them to be fearful in the golden years, and that conflict and criticism probably result from their inability to heal their thinking while young.

I suggest to people when communicating with others, "Say what you mean and mean what you say." Be clear and be certain. Speak with integrity and bring that integrity to your interactions. Not everyone is able to do this. When dealing with people who are out of integrity, your only recourse is to remain steadfast and bring your integrity to every interaction. It will maintain your sanity.

Without forgiveness, we create blind spots. We judge others and aren't aware of the full boomerang effect if we attribute the wrong meaning to what the person in front of has said. You can't see clearly when you can't separate past infractions from current behaviors of someone who wasn't even in your life in the past. Even if the person in front of you doesn't mean to, they may trigger you. You will hear them and feel judged. This new person has no idea what happened to you years ago and may have no malice toward you, but you might feel as if they do.

Someone once asked me if I mistrust people. I said no, which shocked her because she sees me as a person who might think and feel as she does. She is blind to her own creation story, one that says people cannot be trusted. In this case, her inability to forgive is a block, leaving her unable to see and hear people clearly in the present moment. This is another case in which forgiveness can be a key to living freely.

Mind Shift: Forgiveness Journey

Forgiveness is not a one-time actualization, like an accomplishment we can check off a to-do list that signals we are done with the infraction. Forging ahead without forgiving is a trade-off that can come back to haunt you when you least expect it. *Nonforgiveness* creates barriers seeped in resentment, anger, sadness, rejection, and for some, holding back to build revenge.

Our ability to hold on to nonforgiveness is a journey that hurts us. Our bitterness can poison and bleed onto people in front of us who don't have anything to do with person who offended you.

We all want to be forgiven for our mistakes, so it is unfair to be unable to forgive. What are you creating energetically in your body and in your other ongoing relationships by being unforgiving?

This is a good place to list ways to journey through forgiveness:

- To forgive yourself is to acknowledge what you did, determine what you were thinking at that time, and review the scenario and why it was hurtful to others and yourself. The infraction typically originates from emotional pain and causes more. Pain takes time to heal. You know you are making progress when you can see your humanity and that of the other person.
- Open your self-talk to the kindness you desire to receive from others. Your yearning is to achieve acceptance and a pardon.
- Accept what was done and the reactions it caused. Mourn any loss.
- Offer an explanation and honest answers to the questions of the injured party.
- Take deep cleansing breaths, be vigilant with caring self-talk and begin again with the intention to do and be better with your own feelings and decisions going forward.
- Offer the same respect and care as well to others.
- Decide to open your mind and heart to make room for your very own personal peace treaty.

This formula may be repeated as many times as necessary:

1. Document the story of why you have had an inability to forgive yourself for an indiscretion committed by you.

2. Document the story of people you are unable to forgive.

3. Document the story you tell of others who have been unable to forgive you.

4. For stories in Steps 1 through 3, highlight any feeling words. Circle any statements that show you are human.

5. Examine the stories for statements that tear you down or incriminate the offending person in the second and third documents you created.

6. Look for statements you could be imagining by underlining anything you cannot say is factual. For example, you were a child and heard an argument between two adults. The louder, scarier voice came from the male figure, and you were frightened. In your memory, he became the offender. But what if the person in the wrong didn't know what to say in return?

7. What about either of the stories above is repeated to this day with your other interactions with different people? Write two scenarios: *Patterns that make me feel good and I want to keep* and *Patterns that are best for me to let go of*, and write why for both.

8. Write a forgiveness statement for yourself to read based on facts and what you desire to feel going forward from Steps 1 and 2 above.

9. Write a forgiveness statement to the offender from your third story above. Include the objective of how forgiveness from this will free your mind and heart going forward. It could read something like this:

I am forgiving [name of person] *because I desire to be free of holding on to* [feeling] *I have been harboring.*

Feelings being harbored could be hatred, disappointment, hurt, indifference, or being closed off to others as a means of protection. Identifying and releasing what you have been closed off to allows more freedom in your feeling life.

Sometimes a sadness feels so real when we lay down beliefs that had been holding us back. Those beliefs were like a weighted comfort blanket. We get comfortably settled under it because it is all we've known. We exist in the heaviness, and it becomes second nature.

Now that you are trying to take off the weighted blanket, you may feel afraid because life without it is an unknown, and it has been with you for so long. When you have the courage to finally take it off, you feel unrestricted, and that is unfamiliar at the onset. Remind yourself that your desire to live freely, openly, lovingly, joyfully, serenely, kindly, and wisely is greater than the weightiness in a seeming comfort you had been enduring.

We stay in what I term *PHEW* moments, when we are Passionately Holding Even When the thought is not helpful to our higher-living goal. Envision seeing your less-than-powerful thinking as old bones hitting the ground. Each bone is an event from your past. Walk away from those bones as they fall away. Your old thinking does not have to serve as your skeleton any longer.

Cultural Shame: An Old Tool to Fool

Culturally, people have used shame to control others. This happens in our homes and in the world. Tribal lineages can use shame as a tool in our early stages of development. We hear statements such as, "We don't do that in this family," or, "There is something wrong with that—don't do it again!"

Are you tired of feeling shame for something you did or said, or for whom you consider yourself to be?

Behind shame is the belief that we are unworthy of being and belonging in a particular environment. It may be based on something we have done or said. Often it is from so long ago, we don't recall what it was, but we carry it and build mental stories to support it years later in our current situations. Shame needs you to acknowledge and accept what is or has happened. Forgive yourself to see more clearly the various truths surrounding the situation.

If you did or said something deemed egregious, you can move beyond shame by reflecting on your behavior, making an apology, and letting go of the thinking that created the feeling. If the culprit is how you look or whom you love that produces thoughts and feelings of shame, that requires letting go of cultural norms and tribal resolutions to be freely who you came here to be or who you've decided to be. That overhaul to your thinking lays down hatred and fear for a tradeoff of self-acceptance, love, and grace. That grace is extended to yourself and to those who may never understand. It's okay; they do not have to be on board, and you can accept that fact.

Seeking and striving for anything outside yourself to feel worthy is never the answer toward living in your freedom; it is looking in the wrong place for your joy, grace, peace, and freedom. Do you know people who look for their career, more education, a new love interest, or more money to solve their lack of joy?

Joy, grace, and peace are inherent. Seeking validation beyond ourselves creates more angst because external happiness is transient. Happiness isn't sustainable if it depends on others. Joy is intrinsic, and it is how you are meant to feel. When you hold others responsible for making you feel joyful, joy is obscured.

Joy replaces and dismisses depression. Consider depression as the body's way of saying you need a change. What better way to change than shifting your thinking to feel joy in little moments, to amplify that feeling of: *Things are going well?* Depression can also result when you think your life does not look the way it was supposed to based on the creation story you tell yourself or when something is not materializing in the timeframe you deemed appropriate. Remember: *Joy is an inside job.* Things and people are outside you. Those occurrences cannot sustain joy for you.

Seeking *success* to make us feel pumped up feeds a fear that, just by our being on Earth, we are not enough. Get to know yourself, befriend yourself, see your goodness, and let that be your pumped-up sense. That sense of self-worth can take you anywhere to whatever pursuits you are called to do and be.

You want to be president of your own company? Figure out why. If it is to have, let's say, perceived power, to be a multi-millionaire—if the reasons are to alleviate some fear you have, it will backfire, whether you reach the goal or not. If you reach it and still you feel uneasy or unsure of yourself—questioning whether you should be in that position, whether you think you are an impostor—you are living in the fear your soul wants to heal. I have known titans of business who climbed toward the clouds beyond anything their parents thought they could achieve. Yet, they continued to believe they were not worthy of the position. They had achieved the promotion but did not believe themselves worthy of it in their hearts.

The disconnection followed them on every business trip, every round of golf, and every talk they gave because they believed something they were told by those who happened to be imperfect relatives. This is when forgiveness and self-love are needed to clean up the mess from the first aisle in the supermarket of life, where we toiled as young people.

Carrying that misbelief everywhere you go is exhausting and emotionally debilitating. And yet we go out and put on a smile and pretend our way through, rather than stopping to assess whether this line of thinking makes us feel bad or unfulfilled.

Perhaps the real message is:

This line of thinking I have formed is just not true and certainly not creating the life I desire to feel.

Shift your mind to free yourself from worrying about who will guess the secrets you harbor that you aren't nice enough, good enough, you don't like yourself very much, or that you believe you will never live up to the expectations set up by others. This is your feeling inadequate, no matter how much good you have done in the world. Berating yourself does not serve you, nor does it serve the world; believing negative things said about you or people like you keeps you walking in the dark halls of high school. It screams out: *Free your mind from the garbage can!* and *Let's enter the residence of mental freedom!*

Mental freedom is peace, and if you believe in heaven and hell, mental freedom is heaven, and not-good-enough self-thoughts are hell, right here on Earth. Be the president of your own life; lead yourself with integrity and positive self-regard. Being comfortable in your own skin allows you to be comfortable with others and encourages them to be who they are meant to be. That freedom allows everyone to be the best version of themselves. That allows us to solve problems and encourage each other to greater heights.

An important aspect of changing your mind is developing the ability to become still enough to hear your thoughts, which frightens some people. A medical doctor told me she could not quiet her mind to meditate. She had so many thoughts and things to accomplish outside herself; therefore, she could not get to know herself in any other way. Her awareness was derived from her derailed thinking pattern. Her inability to settle her thinking mind perpetuated a fear of not getting it all done or missing important elements of her job. She worried more about what others thought than what was important to maintaining her peace of mind.

Her constant movement and inability to focus created anxiety-thinking that often resulted in loss of time and increased worry, which held her in fear mode. Fear of loss is a sure way of losing your emotional balance, usurping your peace for that which may or may not happen. Placing a premium on losing what she held dear, her reputation based on others' opinions held her hostage to an impending sense of doom. She allowed her fear to rob her of the ability to be in the moment, living freely and honestly.

She and I discussed the fact that everything living changes. Life is not permanent. If you bemoan what once was, you miss what is and are stymied by what is possible. Loss of any type seems so hard for many people.

Remember your first crush, and how you thought you would never recover from that separation, but you did, and now you have a totally different life? You couldn't see it at the time. Which means anything outside you does not have to take you down and put you out of commission for living life and repairing missteps and mishaps.

Our storytelling can be gruesome around the subject of change. It can maintain deep sadness longer than necessary. I'm here to share it does not have to stay that way. Give yourself some slack. No—not slack—give yourself the *love* you are seeking from everybody else. That's when you start exuding the energy level that you want to receive in return.

You're not looking for love; you're not on the hunt for it, you are exuding it, and others get to feel that energy. That's what makes you attractive to be around, at home or work. You are the Master of your Universe; therefore, you get to choose how you want to experience this life.

You Are the Author and Editor of Your Life

If your life is not working for you, stop the story you are telling yourself. Instead, tell a story that says: *We have run our track together long enough, and it stops today.*

You are tired because you know it cannot be true that life should be this hard.

Here's a fact: no one on earth has a forever-perfect life. What we have, though, is the life of our design. So, if your life looks like something you don't desire, you have an obligation and a right to change it. If your life choices and thoughts have made you feel ill, out of sorts, or disheartened, change your narrative. Be your own painter and paint a life that is better. Be your own author and editor and rewrite a better life.

If you've been living this long in internal disarray, why would you think it should fall away in a day? Rewriting and editing takes concentration, diligence, and desire. If you don't have those and you want to remain unhappy and unfit, then you keep writing the same tragic story of *Woe is me*. It does not work to simply pretend to be happy, because the energy behind that pretending is toxic. But if you want to change, start by asking yourself:

- *How have I been benefiting from this line of thinking?*
- *How is this lower energy helping the others in my life?*
- *If I want a better life, why do I continue to embrace the toxicity of my habitual thinking?*

And if you are a grown person who is still blaming your parents, siblings, or guardians for your life not being what you say you want, or for not feeling your best self because of what they said or what they did years ago, you are not taking responsibility for your adult life. You are abdicating your responsibility for the rest of your life. You are blaming people who were doing the very best they could.

Sometimes that best looks sloppy to the adult child, and that keeps you stuck, prolonging the pain you carry daily. Get yourself a good therapist to help you excavate those memories and feelings. Examining their mishaps and mistreatment can help you change the way you see yourself and to identify the self you want to be. Then, every day you wake up and walk out the door, you remind yourself of who you are choosing to be.

Be the best to give the best you have to offer. And if you have children, apologize to them because you have put something in them that they could be holding on to that is affecting their lives. Stop pretending and be real. Real is not: *I am bad,* and *I am negative.* Nor is it: *I am unlovable.* That's not real because if it were real, you would feel good about it. Real is vulnerable.

The narratives we build from our childhood are seen through a child's eyes by someone with so little life experience, they can't possibly figure out what's real and what isn't real. Children are told things that may not be true, and they add those untruths to their narrative. As I contemplate untruths from my past and I talk to my friends who have held on too long to the stories that cloud their judgment about themselves and the world they're living in, it dawns on me that we are wasting time. We are giving away energy to past events we don't even want to remember or relive.

I watched a TV movie about a young woman whose father disappeared before she was able to know him. Her narrative was he never returned, and as such, he didn't love her. She grew older and would ask her mother why he didn't return. The mother would say he didn't want to come back to them. She would say he wasn't ready to be a father. The mother moved on and married someone else, and the three of them built a life together.

The young woman in the story found out later that her father went away not for the reasons her mother thought and shared. This young woman had designed her life around those stores she was told. Now, in the movie, this young woman was able in an instant to let go of those past beliefs, and of course, she fell in love and moved on with her life in that storybook way, the story that makes one think *happily ever after*.

I grew up with stories about a father who abandoned his responsibilities to his daughter's well-being, and from there, I told myself my father loved me so much—yet he was able to walk away. What seems familiar to me in the arena of love was attracting men with that similar energy—the energy that adored me and could walk away. And then I decided to start walking away before they could.

Now that I know the story of my father's leaving was not the story I was telling myself, I must sit with forty-plus years of narrative that wasn't ever true. I get to explore and wonder how I rewrite the story and attract what I truly want. This revelation has been significant, and it sent me into a standstill. What I did know was I wanted to rewrite an honest, loving story about relationships and how that develops, grows, and morphs into my and his highest good.

That, dear reader, is trust. I put one foot in front of the other, day by day, and sometimes hour by hour. I open my heartspace to peace as well as sharing and receiving love. I am receptive always to the greatest gift in that department. I open my heart and eyes to be it and to see it in daily life with total gratitude at the end of each night.

I encourage you to recognize and express your love to your family and friends, and remember to share it with yourself because you matter, and the recognition of mattering is powerful. There is no reason to rehearse, only to trust. No need to overthink yourself back into fear narratives. Once you are free to be yourself, you can see others more clearly, as discussed in the next chapter.

Chapter Six

Seeing People as They Are

Our goal is to see from eyes of grace people beyond their bodies of hurts, as if we are remembering times when we wished someone could see us beyond our worst words and deeds. This is why you make a sincere declaration that you are ready for change.

Our ego—the pesky voice that warns us about everyone and every new thing—wants us to be fearful, so our lives stay small, and we believe the ego's forceful voice is making us safer. There is nothing safe about living small when your soul came here to be something much more expansive. Being closed off in relationships does not guarantee safety from hurt either. Diminishing our possibilities leads to regret and upset. That buildup adds to the past traumas and builds defenses in us that cause us to stay in perpetual levels of discontent and possible anxiety.

Do you want to live with discontentment each day as a means of protection from other people?

No one controls you unless you allow it. You are responsible for yourself and how you show up in your life and interact with others. People will do what they want, and it may not have anything to do with you, just as you are not responsible for what anyone else decides to do in their interactions with others.

Interacting With Others

We live too comfortably accepting numerous situations at face value. Someone is grumpy or says something harsh, and we judge them and slam them for their very existence. This happens in social media, news reporting, corporations, politics, and in our personal interactions. We justify condemnation: *I never did that to anyone*. I suggest we dig deeper to understand people and wait to hear more information.

A parking garage bar would not lift for an employee who wanted to exit the premises. He was recorded hitting the bar with a baseball bat. Not only is this extreme behavior, it's also illegal to destroy property. Outrage and screams ensued that he needed to be fired. No one asked what caused his behavior. No one asked what makes a person overreact to an inconvenience. There is this rush to judgment with videos in particular, with little to no compassion for the possibilities of what we did not see.

When faced with the desire to judge immediately before you have any facts, ask yourself a few clarifying questions to save your blood pressure from rising:

- *What could be happening in that person's life?*
- *What circumstances past or present could be haunting them?*
- *Can I see beyond my immediate reaction?*

We can curb our outrage with practice and patience toward others. I used to be guilty of my thoughts leading me to feel so hurt, I couldn't allow myself to see the other person as having troubles. It used to be when I was tired. I'd go right into the hurt or judgment mode. Since then, I have learned not to speak right away, so I do not have to apologize for any outbursts. I have saved myself from myself and possibly having to retract what I retorted.

This is not a prescription for every situation. Habitual offenders who do not want to change may require a different tactic. For those people, it's best to love them from afar and wish them well. Set boundaries ahead of time that say: *This is what I'm willing to accept and this is what I won't accept.* You do not have to get in the mud with them and match their behavior. If you do, you may feel good for an instant, but tearing another person down wears you down as well. The goal is to uplift yourself that you may be a positive influence for others to observe. Vengeance does not have to be yours.

I am blessed with an ability to see many possible sides of a situation. This ability helps me to understand more than the words people are sharing when I tune in. It also allows me to sense their emotions and, at times, the physical pain they may be experiencing. I am not a clairvoyant, so I can't tell what happened to them in the past, but I can sense that something has happened and stayed within them in this present moment. I can sense when people are off-center, as if their sadness calls to my heart. This is when I decide to be careful, not to take on their sadness, for example. I must remember this is their journey, and my job is to ask questions in hopes their answers will spark some clarity within themselves.

When a statement or situation feels like manipulation, for example, someone is sharing their woe-is-me thinking, I can allow space for them to talk and keep my thinking on the idea that this is part of their journey. I don't need to ride the emotional wave with them because I am capable of deciding for myself whether I want to do or am capable of doing what they are asking.

When their conversation is incongruent, I have learned to ask questions and stand back. When they are lying, either to me or themselves, I recognize if the truth cannot be shared, there must be fear of not feeling loved. Some tell themselves the lie will make them look better in my eyes. There may be a fear of possible consequences; some people will create lies to make themselves feel better in front of others by putting someone else at fault. It is a cry to be seen not for who they are, but for their actions. The illusion they are hoping to pose generally backfires in time.

A Course in Miracles says people you interact with in any situation are either Loving or in need of Loving. This reminds me to keep my thinking clear enough not to let my own thoughts go haywire. Trust me—my thinking may become highjacked; however, with practice, my awareness is swift, and therefore, my rejection of self-harm comes to the rescue. I have recurring themes of doubt that require me to ask myself: *What am I to learn from this?* or *Whom am I to forgive for this situation?*

Self-love, just like any loving relationship with others, requires time, truth-telling, awareness, and patience. We take the time to better ourselves, and thus we can be better as we deal with the people around us who did not or have not taken the time to figure out their own dysfunction. Some people just don't know any better, which gives you the opportunity to be a beacon of light that encourages them to see what being better can look and feel like.

Let us use our internal and learned wisdom and not our frailties to discover how to interact with others without outbursts that shut down communication. We want communication that leads us to better interpret the many possibilities of what could be happening in our conversation. May our and their vulnerabilities be met with love, kindness, and respect. Let us listen with understanding and not merely respond—expect to be filled with energy that we may move comfortably in communication and connections with others.

We are required to meet people where they are on their way to learn about loving, trust, and appreciation. If I see or feel they are plagued by painful thoughts, I will radiate love and accept where they are on their journey. When people can't bear to hear the truth of their magnificence, nor trust the magnitude of that truth, I have learned to be gentle. Love is gentle. It never needs to be forced upon another. Ultimately it is the person's responsibility and desire that help them see their own magnificence.

Fear is forceful and tends to want to exert control over situations and other people. And yet, people miss the point that force does not provide sustainable well-being for either person. *You must do it my way* thinking is forced control that sets up separation, mistrust, and a communication wedge.

I had a boss who insisted his employees do presentation projects his way. I would retreat to my office to do it the way he described what he wanted. I'd present my work to him, only to be asked after he glanced at it, "What is this?"

I would take a deep breath and say, "This is what you asked for."

He'd say, "I didn't ask for this," or on a good day, "I didn't mean this."

At first, I thought he had forgotten what he asked for, and I'd think: *This is unfair!* which led to my feelings of frustration that the presentation was a waste of my time.

It took me a while before I realized he was a visual person who needed to see things written out in order to determine whether he liked it. While I was frustrated, he was requesting what he needed in order for him to decide how he wanted the presentation to look. Before my understanding of what was happening, I was annoyed and considered labeling him a terrible manager. None of that thinking helped me to enjoy our interaction or the task. My taking it personally that something was wrong with me because I didn't provide what he needed was not helping my intelligent light to shine brighter.

If you find yourself in similar situation, it could be that your sensibilities and another's personality may not be a good match. The person may or may not change, and you have no control over that. You can change your perception to find your peace of mind. You decide how you want to process all interactions. That decision can lead to a multitude of solutions. Choose with compassion for yourself and the other person. You do not have to be angry to leave the situation if it is destroying your positive sense of yourself. These situations teach us, once again, not to take in the feeling that something is wrong with us or that something is wrong with the other person. We both likely take in information differently.

Some days I am exhausted by the cruelty people show to each other. The act of bullying assaults my inner being because I can see both people's suffering. I remind myself a person's guilt is their cry for help. A person who misses the loving mark is begging to find their loving self buried so deeply under their hurt and pain, they can't receive or retrieve any original aspect of themselves.

Their thought circuits misfire, and they harm themselves and wound others verbally and sometimes physically. People cry for help in a world that punishes and judges harshly rather than explores the humanity within themselves and in others.

My first and only time serving on a jury was traumatic to my sensibilities, to say the least. I was so traumatized, the other jurors were afraid to let me walk out of the jury room. These are people who didn't even know me, but they could see I was physically and emotionally shaken by the experience. I strongly felt: *Who am I to judge this person when I know nothing of where they come from and what wounds they are carrying?* I understood the concept of punishment for an infraction, and I understood deeply the setup of creating disadvantaged situations for groups of people resulting in desperation and an unhealthy survival mode.

We found the accused guilty of a robbery attempt, and sentencing was set for a later date. As I stumbled to my car and fumbled with my key to unlock the door, I noticed the guilty young man and his girlfriend walking hand-in-hand to their car.

Find another person's humanity by understanding when you have ever done something similar. If someone takes something that is not theirs, the world says they are a thief and should be locked up. If someone steals food to feed their starving child and didn't eat any for themselves, it's now a grey area for some people. When have you ever done something out of integrity? That is a starting point to seeing people as they are.

If you are still judging what they did, you may have a problem forgiving yourself for your impropriety, no matter what it was. Ideally, forgiveness of ourselves helps us to forgive others. Some people say they can forgive others but not themselves.

How has non-self-forgiveness helped you live a more peaceful, more loving, or more joyful, life?

If the answer is: *It has not*, it's your wakeup call to try on new thinking habits to free yourself and to see beyond others' faults as well. We are here on this earth to be happy, to learn, and to reignite the spark of our best self. We sometimes turn away from these rules to make others feel comfortable. We chip away at ourselves to fit in with other people in exchange for fitting in with ourselves.

You came here to be you, and you are the only person capable of fully being you. No one else can command authority over you unless you give them permission by acquiescing to their demands without regard to your own needs and desires.

When you are feeling disgruntled by people's energy, take several deep, cleansing breaths—a deep breath in, notice your stomach pokes out, hold for a few seconds, and let the breath out. Notice your stomach points toward your ribcage—and remind yourself you have no idea what they have been through or what they are currently going through.

Being hurtful is not anyone's complete identity. They may be in a hurting space for this moment, and your kindness may help them. Treat them as you would want someone to treat you if they didn't know the circumstances of your life when you were in an unpleasant mood. See their infraction through less resentful eyes, and you are freer in your mind and your body.

You are inherently capable of letting go of someone else's issues. Allow yourself to see the scenario differently, so you might not have to hold on to the disgruntled feelings for any length of time. I do recommend asking yourself what you might learn from your triggers. That awareness can assist you in the process of healing your emotional wounds. We learn more about ourselves in relationship with others. Their behavior becomes a mirror to our reactions. I share with coaching clients that, many times, the people who offend us the most are the gift-givers essential in achieving our emotional healing goals.

If you say to yourself: *I don't let people in to protect myself from hurt*, you are projecting onto them and creating the energy for exactly what you get: hurt. When various relationships in our lives disappoint us, we must learn how to process and move beyond our old ways of handling our dismay. Relationships discontinue, lies are uncovered, and hurt ensues. The hurt causes us to believe the other person was unjust in their treatment of the relationship. I wonder if the offensive behavior feels so bad because of residual hurt from past relationships gone awry.

Are you stewing in your past hurt and dragging it into your current situation?

Could it be time to create different scenarios as you draw new people into your life?

Give people space to be who they think they are, and then act accordingly when there is a boundary issue. I have been guilty of presupposing someone will do the wrong thing. But here's what I have learned that I hope will be helpful to you: Every person I have had to let go I have missed, I have cried for what would no longer be, and I have wished them well because I also want to be well. Hard feelings abate, we grow, and we move on—no ill will, no judgment. That gives you space to create new and better-suited relationships.

Sabotage – A Closer Look

You might sabotage relationships, not solely because of you and how you are; it's often also because of your self-doubt or lack of personal awareness. I am talking about you and me as well as all the other people we encounter in our daily life, whether it's in the workplace or school settings, churches, or home. Other people's sabotage doesn't let you or me off the hook.

We must look at our own messy thoughts and feelings to understand:

- Whether we have ever sabotaged a relationship
- Why we attract that energy into our lives
- Why we held on too long
- Why we repeat the scenario
- What we are to learn about ourselves
- What we are willing to change for a different outcome
- Beliefs we hold that are not in our best interest
- What we hold on to that we would benefit from forgiving ourselves and not revaluating

When you focus on the future, such as believing you can be happy only with a certain job or person in your life, you make your life a little harder. Or, have you ever said, "I won't be able to live or feed myself or my family without *this* current situation?"

This is you giving your power to something outside yourself. The ego will say: *I am protecting you; stay and work harder to get a promotion, and then you will feel happy.* The truth is once you achieve those outer things, your ego still won't be satisfied. It wants you to strive for something else. It keeps you moving and seeking because you won't be able to take time to see your authentic self is enough without any outer trimmings.

I advocate self-reflection and creating a plan to get more of what you want without letting the current situation rob you of your true gifts and health. We get stuck in telling ourselves: *I will keep the devil* (job, person, living arrangement) *I know*. Our authentic self knows we are capable of doing well in environments that respect and honor our gifts and talents. Without the ego, you learn a title doesn't give you sustainable power. Your real authority originates from living in integrity, cultivating insight, and loving yourself and others. That is where your real power comes from. If you are displeased with the job, family members, or any other interactions, determine which comes first: cultural change or personal change? Hint: it's the one where you have dominion.

If you are a rule-follower or a people-pleaser, this is a difficult concept. People will say: *I do a good job, and I just want to be recognized for it.* That is reasonable, right? We desire to be rewarded for our contributions. However, if your boss is putting value on things you do not do or offer, they may compensate someone who delivers what they value. The boss in this situation may be rewarding others without considering your strengths and gifts. For example, a boss who values employees who are rebels (because the boss can't be perceived as a rebel) will not be able to praise or fairly compensate a rule-follower. A boss who is a rebel may not understand the value a people-pleaser/rule-follower brings to the table.

If your life goals are not working out, if you are struggling to be your best self, if people who love you are ready to give up on you, it may not mean anything negative about you. You may think yourself into believing you feel like a disappointment. It could be happening because it's time for you to support yourself first. People may need to get out of the way so you can find your happiness hallmark and self-sufficient space and experience your most loving life.

Sometimes you must let go of things or people to retrieve your real self. When you are empowered to be your truest, most positive, and loving self, you also provide a safe place for others to be their true selves. That is the standard to strive toward daily. Share what you learn with others to help them improve their life. Surprise people with your safe-to-be-you-in-my-presence stance, especially when others aren't expecting it.

This is not a recipe for giving in to other people's dilemmas or their imposing standards and expectations. This is a recipe for shining your brightest internal light and leaving behind enough grace that someone else may want to shine their light brighter than what they have shown you before. Our best self can set us up for the next step, leaning in to our responsibility in our interactions and allowing us to see other people as they choose to be.

Chapter Seven

Your Relationship
With the World

L et's explore within us what is required to develop personal responsibility in relationship within the world.

I learned from the great thought leader and deceased inspirational author, Wayne Dyer, to keep my eyes on my desire and to keep my heart open to what I am meant to do in this world, so my gifts can be felt by others. It ensures my gifts do not evaporate once I depart this Earth. Our foundational ideas, grounded in love and sharing, may appear to dissipate; however, our shared messages will continue with the people we have poured into.

That translates to: Share the greatest of who you are. There is no one exactly like you, and that is no mistake. You were and are wonderfully made. Your loving self, who you truly are, needs be shared with the world. To do so, pay close attention to the whispers within you to learn what you are on Earth to do. Your soul is trying to remind you it is your mission to share your gifts with others.

For my dear readers who say: *I don't hear anything*, instruct your mind it's time to put the longstanding useless chatter to rest. Do not allow your mind to wallow in thoughts that hold you hostage to avoid what is truly calling your attention.

Exercise: Hearing From Your Heart

Practice quieting your mind:

- Take deep breaths as discussed in Chapter Three, *Mind Shift: Be Present*.
- Revisit your childhood wonders and curiosities and create a list of what intrigued you.
- What compliments did you receive when you were younger that continue today?
- Remember what that felt like, and walk around with that good feeling, so the voice inside your mind becomes reacquainted with the feel of a higher vibration.
- As you feel the higher vibration, jot down those small whispers that are reminders of what you can share.
- As the thoughts get louder and more persistent, continue writing them down.
- Determine how can you insert these messages in everyday interactions, such as encouraging others or offering your personal gift freely to anyone who has need, expecting nothing in return.

When I repeatedly completed the above exercise, I realized I had always relied gratefully on my grandmother's love and acceptance of me exactly as I was. I carried that feeling of acceptance into my career in

Corporate America. That knowing set a tone for my interactions with managers. I met them feeling like a competent person. A few managers and coworkers in the early days tried to impose on my demeanor. Those were some tough days, and I could feel myself shrink. I had to strengthen my resolve daily so as not to become hostile and bitter. I decided I would not allow them to shake my energy. I knew my inner competence to understand concepts and to think through next steps. My primary goal was to do a good job and get a good annual salary increase.

I had to learn to discern when their critique was helpful and when it was designed to deflate me. I have wanted to be a writer since my freshman year in college.

One of my earlier bosses would tell me regularly: *You don't write well.* She couldn't articulate what was wrong, she just didn't like my style. She declared, "You just don't have what it takes."

This was crushing to me because I desperately wanted to be an author one day. I had to teach myself to see through her messages to understand her concern and discern her fears, which enhanced her need to control without regard to offering how to improve. This awareness helped me to not take the words or treatment personally. It was also a first clue I needed to move my career along and away from her management style.

Fast-forward years later, I was working with another manager who red-lined a proposal I wrote that was going to senior management. I was immediately emotionally high-jacked back to the earlier career incident. I was hurt and visibly upset. I had to take a walk to calm myself. I went home that evening and tried to understand what was happening. Was my writing truly that awful?

I looked at each of her comments, and I realized I could make the proposal sound stronger and clearer. Unlike the first boss, this one was helping me by citing why changes were needed. I became energized and began rewriting that evening. She wanted me to look professional in front of senior management. She wanted to pull the best out of me and teach me at the same time. I will forever be grateful for the hard-learned lesson. The feedback from the senior manager: it was the best proposal he had read, and it was approved for funding.

My boss had helped me tap back into my self-assurance, which had been whispering to me since college. I had to believe fully in my ability. When we take our self-assured energy wherever we go, it is felt by those with whom we come into contact.

Another important aspect of relating to the world around us is self-acceptance. It is authentic living to accept our strengths and our insecurities. In my mid-adult years, I realized in other relationships I had attracted and been attached to similar feelings of love my parents provided as best they could. I observed my parents closely, feeling their exchanged energy. When they were not in a pleasant phase, I would do whatever I could to make them laugh or provide hugs to shake the mood.

I no longer try to fix my difficult and disappointing interactions with laughter or conjoining. I remind myself people can have an ego at work within them. It's important, therefore, to ask myself, "Who is showing up in my various interactions, my ego, or my authentic self?" The authentic self can admit hurt feelings or vulnerability. The authentic self is looking for a win-win for our potential to grow in relationships and individually.

The ego is concerned with being perceived as right. Feeling your adult wholeness is the recognition that childhood experiences don't have to continue to control your way of thinking or to continue to hurl your feelings into sadness or discomfort.

When you are tired of the past directing your present, you seek to change your way of being in relationships. This is an ongoing journey. Just when you think you have conquered one aspect of a childhood pain point, a long-forgotten one shows up with its hand waving for attention and healing. Our insecurities require examination, and they can benefit from adjusting our thinking because *adulting* is an ongoing adventure in self-discovery.

In my grandmother's presence, I felt loved for who I was, just because I was here on Earth. I felt her delight. We could talk to each other like no others in the family. I could say things her own children weren't allowed to or were afraid to say. I realize love energy needs to be taken into all relationships. No more watching and weaving stories based on negative past experiences or betrayals. I am myself, who always allows others to be their selves, as they so choose. That's the energy I strive to take with me into the world.

Letting go of watching and evaluating and storytelling my interactions with others requires me to be my perfectly imperfect self, without fear of abandonment. An absent father can affect a little girl well into her mature years. The imprint can bring up hurt and mistrust at work and in other areas in one's life. This is when we turn to a Divine energy for internal fortitude and the ability to grow beyond childhood wounds.

What do you need to release in relationships, based on the behaviors you saw in the environment in which you grew up?

When you decide what behaviors you have adopted that serve neither you nor your relationships well, you may be more willing to think and do your part to create connecting energy for more satisfying relationships within your chosen group of people.

Now, for those of you who can only remember the teasing, hurtful, and painful times in your young or current life, the above question does not have to feel difficult. I know your head is racing, and likely your thoughts are telling you all manner of stories, such as: *No one liked me*, or it's saying: *The people who pretended to like me really weren't kind; they would leave me and that would hurt.*

I have a suggestion: List what you wish they had seen and known about you. Show that part of yourself to the world.

If you consider yourself a natural-born giver, but you feel you don't get anything in return, that thought process might weigh you down. It's time to make a shift in how you give. Only give what you have inside that does not ask for anything in return. That releases you from manipulating and lessens the thoughts that their return effort is never as good as you would hope.

If changing from being an over-giver is too frightening for you to change on your own, seek a competent behavioral therapist to help you make changes and see yourself in a different light. The goal is to shine your brilliant light in the world. Make a difference, not for your ego's satisfaction, but to help spark generations around you.

The ego-voice sounds authoritative, as if it were a separate entity from all your other critical thinking and feeling. It sounds off in your head as if it is your sense of who you are in this world and dictates how you must show up in protection mode. It is not concerned with your deeper need for peace and connection. Rather, it is critical and ferociously repetitive to ensure it holds your attention.

Ego can take on the guise of self-protection when it is actually betraying your best interest. It can be cunning, telling you, "Listen to me, and I will tell you what and who to watch out for, so you do not fall prey to more hurt." When you trust the ego-voice, it tells you to believe people's current motives are similar to those of your past interactions and fears. It will even go so far as say in your mind, "You are wrong if you begin to think loftier thoughts about yourself and your abilities."

The ego-voice holds you in despair, fear, pain, and self-loathing to control you. As a result, you may then try to control situations and others. The voice of ego is not purpose-driven and is certainly not loving. We have listened to it for so long, we think it is our truth, lovingly trying to protect us. As you awaken to your true self, you can see clearly your ego does not have to run your life any longer.

The people around you need to see your humanity, your love, and your kindness. You become the role model for living in awareness and sharing light rather than judgment. Your goals change from wanting to be the only one to win no matter what it takes to wondering how we can all win. Let the next generations watch how life can unfold peacefully and naturally without compromising themselves.

The Unfamiliar Feeling of Change

Be aware: Change feels uncomfortable because it is unfamiliar territory. Living with internal dissatisfaction is also uncomfortable and grows to being unbearable. The prolonged discomfort is nature's way of saying we need a change. Snakes shed their skin. While the skin is moving over their eyes, they're blinded for a few seconds. This is a metaphor for change in our lives: it feels uncomfortable, but it's necessary to see our higher levels of selfhood.

If snakes turn you off, let's look instead at the butterfly's transition from a small egg into a caterpillar. The caterpillar disintegrates, literally liquifies, and transforms into a chrysalis. To break the shell of the chrysalis, it must go through a "mega-change" or *metamorphosis*, becoming the beauty we witness when we see it flutter in its full embodiment of self-expression.

Infants grow into young children, teens, and adults. At some point, we go through our own metamorphosis when we realize we have let society rule our thinking and belief systems for far too long. We accept, after years of inner turmoil, it's time to push forward into a stronger sense of authentic self-appreciation and new creation. That is what I know is possible within you for your best self-growth and for those around you to see and experience.

With that very understanding, I became ready and able to shift from walking on eggshells to keep peace in relationships. There was no trying to prove my worth through seeking others' approval. The shift was to being accepting and expecting love energy like my grandparent gave to me—one of acceptance and caring. I've learned to say the difficult things from a loving voice rather than being harshly critical.

Look for that initial energy of best love from whoever was there for you in early years. Emulate those who were accepting of you and were delighted to see you and to listen to you. Relax into that energy feeling. This could have been a neighbor, coach, teacher, or your best friend's mother. When you practice this often, the old concept of struggle-love doesn't have to be continued. You won't go searching only to relive your past understanding of pseudo-love. You grow and decide to live more abundantly in love energy that attracts supportive people by your side, people who are excited to see who you are and what you want to become.

When we make relationships so intense they are an indictment of our being, we can forget to live in our own power center. When I have given too much of myself, I find a need to steal away to return to my center. I listen for a sense of clarity and peace within myself first, then turn toward meaningful relationships. The clarity I seek and feel most of the time is what resonates with others.

I feel sad when I realize so many of us spend a lifetime looking for another's love to put us back together or to make us feel whole again, as if someone else's acceptance will do that for us. The truth is we can only do it for ourselves because our best self was established within at the point of creation. We arrive fully as our sweet-loving selves, but we forget quickly as we try to adapt to the outside world's expectations, such as conforming to rules and regulations and cultural expectations. It is a race against pleasing others and self-love awareness. Stop running the external race and embrace your internal self-regard and your special gifts that are to be shared with your fellow travelers in small or large radii of your choosing.

Uncovering Your Personal Best

Here's a framework for the deep dive into the next set of questions: Identify what you believe and allow yourself to experience that today is partly manifested because you created this reality, rather than allowing your ego to scream: *No way did I create this reality! The slights I feel at work are real. The things teachers said to me hurt!*

I understand it hurts when you believe deep inside there is truth to what they have said. If you don't believe what you were told, you could shake it off easily because you don't believe it to be true. In other words, people hurt our feelings *with our given permission*.

Exercise: Personal Probing Questions

The powerful questions for your further exploration are:
- What about you is holding you back from what you desire?
- What are your deepest fears?
- What thoughts do you carry that align with the energy that is holding you back?

To uncover these answers, be thoughtful, reflect on what you have seen in your life that causes you to deny who and what you want. Be patient with yourself. The power is in understanding and accepting you are empowered to change.

This kind of growth requires listening to yourself and acting accordingly, to honor what is best for you. This is not an excuse to bellow in anger; that's the fear model. Self-empowerment says: *This situation is not serving my highest good, and therefore, I'm going to remove myself from this particular situation or ideology.*

This is self-empowerment because you didn't ask anyone's permission to leave or to do something differently. You checked in with your highest self and decided you don't have to twist yourself to be what you are not. Or you could decide to stay, but you want to initiate boundaries. In that case, use self-empowerment statements, such as "I understand how you feel and that we don't agree on this. I say we table this conversation for now." If the person keeps talking, you don't have to engage because you've stated how you feel, or you state, "I want more time to reflect before I can discuss this subject again." You return to the conversation when both of you are ready to go forward.

Marginalization Mystique

The Marginalized Mystique occurs when we seek or allow others' opinions of us to matter so greatly, we hand over our power to make decisions to them. Some take over consciously, fully aware of what they're doing, and rationalize why they need to be in charge of our life. Others of us may allow ourselves to be marginalized unconsciously. We abdicate to others how they wish us to live, no matter the mental and physical toll it takes on our being and body. Giving that power away is harmful to our emotional well-being.

What good can come when so many of us are running around looking for someone else to define us, to determine our worthiness? It only leads to an increased feeling of being outside our own ability to feel happiness. Bowing to other opinions leaves us feeling and being devalued or fearful of others' responses. We are caught in their web.

I was in South Africa talking separately with several generations—an older Black gentleman, a middle-aged Indian man, and a young colored person who witnessed the end of the Apartheid movement—who were affected by the 1948 to 1994 government's enforced Apartheid. After those conversations, I am doubly committed to the message in this book about the effects of the marginalization game.

The South African National Party at the time was an all-white government who handed down a decree that non-white South Africans were required to live in separate areas away from white people. Locations were designated for four different racial groups, Black, white, Indian, and Colored—people of mixed racial blood lines. This separation forcibly uprooted three groups of people from their homes and sent them to places with varying degrees of deprivation. For example, Blacks were sent to shack structures or *shanties* with no indoor bathrooms or electricity. Their voting rights were taken away, and they were forbidden to use public facilities or to go to beaches.

The younger person that witnessed the destruction of Apartheid shared with me his generation developed the understanding that you mustn't believe someone else can define you. You must learn for yourself your own goodness and accept your worthiness to be in any situation of your choosing. Put that message in your mind and embrace it well enough that it lives in your every heartbeat. With that understanding, no one can marginalize your thinking because you don't fit in. Neither does it facilitate condemning others to try to create perceived external power.

You can work for someone who is forceful and controlling and not give your power away. You can see through to their weakest realities and not buy into their obscure messages of separation and division as to who is a better employee than someone else.

The Marginalization Mystique is a con game that people either know they are participating in, or they observed it while growing up and believe it to be the normal order of their living. They subscribe to it and make others believe they are inferior, as if the rules were created only for the oppressors. Any creation that holds others back is rooted in fear and creates havoc. This happens in any and every arena: government, schools, work environments, group settings in religious organizations, the arts, and with creatives. Be aware, because it can happen subtly, and it can happen to any one of us.

Equally as important to counter marginalization is your self-awareness. No one can make you less-than without your consent. They may put down your inner beauty; however, that does not make them right. That makes their actions manipulative. That creates a power hunger within them that is rationalized at any cost. I have heard them say they are just doing what needs to be done to feed their family. As if someone else isn't worthy of feeding themselves or their family.

Here's an incident that taught me marginalization happens in all settings. I was in an upscale store, talking to a salesperson, and I shared that I liked the lip gloss, but felt there was a flaw in the bottle design because the lip gloss leaked out. I asked her would she tell her management. She said I would be better off writing a note and sending it in because management never listens to the sales team when they share what their customers are saying.

What a missed opportunity for management, not to listen to the frontline workers who are dealing directly with customers. Not only is it a missed product improvement opportunity, but it also sends signals to frontline people that they are not valued. Marginalizing people is a construct to keep them from experiencing and expanding their genius. It hurts productivity and the bottom line. I stopped using the product and told of my incident to anyone I knew who used lipstick.

People who are dismissive are attempting to keep you from seeing the truth of your being, your specialness, and your unique gifts. If they can extinguish those qualities in you, they can manipulate and control you in numerous situations. Stop believing what others tell you about who you are. Define your best self, identify your greatest gifts, and share those gifts with no expectations. Feel comfortable in your own skin.

In corporate settings I have overheard people say, "Well, they"—the others who don't look like the speaker—"don't think like us," or "don't sound like us; therefore, we can't promote them as easily as we can people who are like us." They stymie people's creativity and miss by a mile the ability to grow in new and exciting ways within the business as well as to grow human being potential.

Exist Inside Out

We become confused when we think something or someone outside us will bring us peace. Outer attainment and achievement are not a guarantee of lasting peace. If it were, the billionaires would have no problems. The beautiful people would float through life. The only people floating through life are the ones who realize peace is personal awareness that lives inside them, ready to be shared.

Peace is the energy of beaming hearts shining within that illuminate outward. The sun shines daily, even when we can't see it behind the grey clouds. We can remember that peace is in us even when our thinking takes us down a path of want and desire. Peace is an understanding feeling that reassures us when we don't have exactly what we think we deserve or want. Peace is personal. We are more powerful than we know in this moment. Things work out, so there is little need to worry and fret just because you don't know the exact way just yet.

Self-love breathes value into your life and personally touches the lives of others. You decide whether what you're currently doing creates positive value in your life. If yes, keep doing it and enjoy your effect in the world. If no, or there is a caveat to your answer, examine why you are continuing to do that which does not create the value you want to give to the world. Discover what is your payoff.

For example, are you not getting enough sleep because you decide to stay awake and scroll social media? Let's say it helps you to zone out at the end of the day before going to sleep; then that's your value statement. You would rather get caught up on the videos of others' lives, lose track of time, and risk the blue light keeping you up longer. Now if you need more sleep to feel clearheaded in the morning, let that be your value statement and act accordingly. You can set a timer for a limited time to pursue social media. We can learn a lot from good content on social media, but let's not forget corporations are making money by keeping you attached to it longer than might be helpful to your well-being. That too is a form of marginalizing and manipulating you.

My desire to watch daytime TV at home is generally high. When I'm away from home, I don't even think about watching daytime TV, and I do not miss it. The value, I told myself, was I could learn something new about a celebrity or about health by watching daytime TV at home. It could give me something to talk about with others. It was a way to pass time. But did it provide high value to my well-being or to my life? Did I have things to talk about when I was away from daytime TV? *Yes, of course,* I thought. But after some reflection, I realized the answer was *no, it was not giving me the value I thought I prized.*

Reflect on what eats up your time. If you have no immediate answer, take a close look at how you use your daily time. The way you live your life shows you what you value, because you are accountable and capable of creating that life or something better.

If you are not abiding by your foundational values, you flounder and you open yourself up to letting others define what is right for you. You can lose sight of who you are and what is important to you.

Exercise: Setting Values for Well-Being

To identify your time wasters, get a pen and paper or record on your phone. Close your eyes. Take three deep breaths. Open your eyes and ask the questions below. Do not try to clean up your answers so they sound better. Just download the answers on paper or record. Get all the answers out of your head before you examine what you wrote.

- *What did I spend my time on today?* (Do not judge the first thoughts that come to mind.)
- *What's good about what I've recorded?*
- *Do my actions align with my value system?*
- *Do my choices support my values?*
- *How do they align within my values for well-being?*
- *How do they not suit my well-being?*

I value keeping my body strong. That involves what I eat and how I move my body. If I have the time to sit for hours and watch TV, I can surely find time to move my body. I decided during commercials, I would stand and run in place or dance. I sit down after the commercial, but sometimes, I feel comfortable standing and walking in place while the show is on as well. Moving my body is a value that promotes health. I created a way to get it into my daily routine without focusing on excuses of why I could not.

Countering Culture

Traditionally our encounters with culture are counter to knowing our best self. When we are not allowed to demonstrate who we are and do not feel safe doing so, we suffer. Our happiness is, in part, contingent on recognizing that which is counter to cultural norms.

I am responsible for sharing my inherited gifts with the world, as is every person globally—not what our culture says we need to be, nor what anyone outside ourselves says. We can do one thing: show up with our gift. Wherever I go, whether in a corporate setting or with friends and acquaintances, I show my curiosity; I lean in and listen, and I ask thoughtful questions. That seems to be one of my inherited gifts.

Real Love has no requirements or expectations in Humanity Love. That type of Love is what you give or put into yourself and the world. If I say *good morning* to a stranger on the street and they don't say hello back, I don't get upset and curse them silently. My love-greeting was given freely with no strings attached, and I have no need to receive anything in return.

At work, extend kindness to coworkers with no need for their approval and no predetermined need for them to appreciate it or you in a prescribed way. Understand: people who are unkind are likely dealing with something about which you have no idea.

One client complained about the treatment she was receiving from a coworker in her department. Her coworker would call and complain about the lack of attention her concern was given. Nothing seemed reasonable or to her liking. I suggested she should not take her coworkers' behavior personally because that would block the energy she'd need for true connection. I also suggested the two women meet for coffee with the goal of understanding what her coworker was needing rather than why she was behaving negatively.

Through connection, my client learned her coworker's daughter was schizophrenic. The client was divorcing her husband who was demanding a large amount of her money that she needed for her daughter's care in a private facility. The soon-to-be ex-husband wanted nothing to do with the child, so his need for the money was more self-focused. That conversation helped my client create a connection and provide attention and assistance the coworker needed. That was a lesson in how to counter the culture the client thought she was experiencing. She had convinced herself the coworker was out to get her and felt it was personal, even though they didn't know each other well.

We are all people doing the very best we can, sometimes in very difficult circumstances.

- How does that feeling of mistrust creep in and affect how you see and treat others?
- How does your disdain for another person color the effects of your everyday life?

Our inability to forgive, show mercy, or give grace to another based on the stories we tell ourselves about that person becomes our inability to support ourselves. What we cannot do for another we cannot do for ourselves because the energy between us is reciprocal. There is very little internal peace without love and grace for ourselves and others. There may be a tarp lying over the pain, anger, or sorrow, but the pain leaks like methane gas when we do not address what is happening. We need awareness and a decision to resolve the behavior of mistrust.

We need to be the architect of our life going forward. So much seems to have happened throughout our lives. We can mentally enforce our spiritual personal power tools throughout the day. It is time to focus on our life and loving as a good-to-great campaign. I hope and trust you decide to become the architect of your life.

Your brilliance lives in acceptance and gratitude for the gifts inside you. Your gift can be making the most delicious brownies. Your gift can be helping those in less fortunate situations. Your gift can be making others smile as you walk away because you gave them your attention. Your gift can be helping a younger person recognize what is wonderful about them.

May your lost voice return to life and matter mightily for good in the world.

Activities List

Chapter Five

Chapter Seven

Acknowledgments

This book is a love offering to encourage those who have set aside honoring their uniqueness and sharing their inherent gifts in a world that needs what they have to share. The birthing of this book would not have been possible without the following people who gave me kindness, patience, encouragement, and their time and energy, for which I am most appreciative:

Capucia Publishing Team, without out your support, knowledge, expertise and caring, this project would have taken me much longer to complete. Christine, congratulations are in order for all you do to inspire transformational encouragement and for employing such a caring mission. David, you brought me back from a couple of brinks and helped me get out of my head and back into my heart. Great thanks for the work you do in the mindset evolution. Jean Merrill and Carrie Jareed, you both were so encouraging, patient, and in my book (pardon the pun), all-knowing to my many questions. Simon Whaley, your understanding and knowledge of the writing craft, the author's journey, social media, editing, and what titles sound good were by far the best coaching I have received in this space. I so appreciate your candor and assistance. I will follow and support your writing journey always. Ellen Landsburg Monsees and Penny Legg, I learned so much from you both. I could ask any question and you had suggestions for me. You introduced me to new ideas and books that will be helpful throughout my writing career. You are both treasures. Heather Taylor, your suggestions made me think and made me better. Much appreciated.

To my pre-readers, Patricia Evans, Nina Jagannathan, and Amy Riggins, your encouragement, your suggestions, and your unwavering support are forever appreciated. Your thoughts, comments, and recommendations made the finished book better. Thank you!

To my Sisters, Friends, and Daughters of my Heart, your ongoing outpouring of love and acceptance and belief in my abilities to write this book makes me shine brighter and try harder. Thank you: Angela, Aesha, Beth, Connie, Carm, Marguerite, Moni, Kymberli, and Val.

To all my grandchildren by blood and heart-adoption, I adore you and appreciate your existence in this world. Your beings are beauty and greatness. These qualities live inside you and your only job is to share them with others through what you love to do and through what you know to be, which is kind—to yourself and to others. What we gift to the world is what we ultimately gift to ourselves. Share freely with the world; it needs your best selves.

To Honey, Ozzie Smith Jr., your unwavering support, encouragement, and compliments help me to be better.

Emotional Digest

There is power in identifying your emotions and how you have created them. Naming your feelings facilitates identifying where you'd like to go as well as changes you'd like to make. This is essential to elevating yourself to higher levels of purposeful living. You can add to this list other feelings you discover. Share your word and a definition along with an example of how it affects your thoughts on my website, deborahliverett.com.

Abandonment: Sense of being left by other(s) without resources or companionship and, at times, the lack of understanding why it happened.

Agape: Ultimate expression of your soul. It is love with no judgment. It is the sky-level energy emotion, filled with love, joy, and gratitude.

Anger: Fear of being attacked physically or emotionally. Your thoughts look for examples to keep the anger going, and the adrenal glands release hormones throughout the body to help the anger stay alive in you. Justified anger is accepted by the body. Anger is a lower-energy emotion in that it cannot sustain or fuel you for long-term solutions. If you start a project because you feel something unjust happened, you will need additional intentions to keep going, as the anger may fade. If you hold on to anger that is not justified, such as a false judgment of another person, that anger will turn on your body and create dis-ease from within.

Anxiety/Anxiousness: Feelings of uncertainty, excessive concern without a targeted focus. Feelings of tension and worry. Also, nervousness, restlessness, or tenseness. Long term it can present as a sense of impending doom, danger, or panic with no empirical data to support it. Anxiety can be a coverup for anger. Irrational anxiety requires examination. In anxiousness, cortisol pushes with great speed throughout the body. You may feel nervous, restless, or tense. People's bodies behave differently: sweating, troubled breathing, trembling, tiredness, weakness, or an inability to concentrate.

Bliss: State above happiness; great joy that is oblivious of what is happening around you, including other people's drama. Bliss takes on a state of knowing contentment, embracing your internal wisdom, understanding you are secure and living in a peaceful awareness in and of the Divine. Bliss encompasses our energy, emotions, and our two beings: spiritual and physical.

Bitterness: Evokes disappointment and anger when you feel you have been unjustly treated. It can build into resentment if not attended to. It may indicate a need to repair your mental construct of what happened. Unattended bitterness can affect how you interact with others. It can take you hostage if you do not resolve how you let the offense affect you.

Bother: Displaying behavior akin to annoyance, agitation, and aggravation toward others you perceive as an offender of something egregious. If not attended to, it can bleed over into interactions with people not associated with the offending act.

Calmness: A relaxed mind and nervous system. Being free of strong (irritating) emotions.

Compassion: Higher understanding of the *why* behind your reaction, response, or circumstance; a heartfelt desire to help your or others' states of being.

Confusion: Demonstrated when your mind is unclear, and you cannot find a clear solution. The mind is troubled, and therefore, the thoughts and ensuing conversations are disjointed and bewildering. In confusion, it is difficult to make a rational decision. Being confused for too long can create anxiety, stress, depression, and fatigue.

Connection: Human connection thrives in you when you are feeling seen, heard, and valued while interacting with others. The existence of connection creates strong trust bonds and a sense of belonging. Ideally it starts at home and builds into relationships beyond the initial home environment. When you feel connected, you easily deliver your best self. Without connection, the relationship crumbles or exists in separate silos.

Courage: Acting against being scared; showing bravery when the outcome is unknown and could be less than favorable.

Depression: Repressed emotions about what you thought your life would be versus where it is in this moment. A misperception in your thinking produces the notion you are depressed. For example, repressing anger develops into a feeling of being hopelessly depressed. Wanting life to be different than what you perceive it to be.

Disguised Disgust: Shows up as annoyance when you are talking in a meeting or while out with acquaintances, and you think no one hears you because no one responds to what you have said, as if they weren't listening, until a couple minutes pass and you hear someone repeat what you said as if it were their idea. You respond in a terse manner and laugh it off as being playful.

Devastation: Feeling destroyed and distraught emotionally and mentally. It's a profound, overwhelming sense of sadness. Can be felt in the moment when something important is ruined and seems unsalvageable. You want to change but don't know how initially.

Disappointment: When your expectations are not met you can feel disappointment, which can present as complex other feelings, such as sadness, discomfort, frustration, embarrassment, and even anger.

Distrust: Rather than an emotion, distrust and trust are perceptions. Distrust develops from a sense of lack or perceived judgment that something will not happen in your favor. It's a pre-feeling before an event or hope or request.

Empathy: Allows you to hear what is said by another and sense what they must be feeling, even if it does not match their words or outward appearance. You hear the meaning behind their words from deep within. It may provide you with understanding the unconscious meaning of the person you are talking to.

Enthusiasm: Inspired excitement akin to joy, used to start and push forward in a goal. It's a higher-within energy source used to accomplish a desire.

Excitement: Powerful and often fleeting emotion, often associated with new explorations, awareness, or people. Adrenaline courses through your veins when excitement is felt.

Fear: Powerlessness, feeling frightened, terrified, scared. Constricted thinking; lacks a foundation of possibility. Self-condemnation; self-loathing. Fear can motivate you to be still or to propel yourself through what is happening around you. It can move you forward or shrink you; it is always your decision how you will respond to your fear. It elevates the heart rate.

Fluster: Feeling out-of-sorts and not confident.

Frustration: Continually waiting for a change or specific outcome that eludes existence; unmet desires.

Fulfillment: Sense of accomplishment that has served a meaningful purpose.

Fury: Extension of extreme anger.

Gratitude: Acknowledged appreciation.

Grief: Personal array of fluid emotions, such as disbelief, despondent, denial, debilitated, anger, profound sadness.

Guilt: Self-punishment; judgmental assertions generally misplaced. Void of compassion for self.

Happiness: Temporary feeling; fleeting and difficult to sustain when attached to outside sources, such as things, people, purchases, or places. Happiness is fleeting excitement, typically about an incident or accomplishment that is deemed good.

Hate: Belief that someone or something is less-than by your standard; a distorted mindset of separation and unequal; prejudgment of others or judgment of all based on a past negative expression; often passed down by cultural norms, including families/religions. It can create covert and overt hostilities. A sense of intense dislike and distrust. There is a toxic-energy feel to encounters with hate.

Hurt: Discomfort; feeling verbally attacked; inflicted with mental or physical abuse.

Inspiration: Infusing the mind and emotions toward connections with self and others to create new possibilities that can motivate you and others.

Irrational: Other side of clear thinking and thoughtful behaving. When you present out of fear that is not aligned with what is happening in that moment, typically because you were triggered, you can present as irrational.

Joy: Mindset that sustains inner peace, no matter what is happening around you. A trust that everything works for a reason. You may not see it right away, but you trust all will be well. It's the byproduct of a spiritually led existence. To be joyful is to embody motivation, peace, delight, and gratitude in the moment. You carry it inside you like a secret ingredient you share with your presence.

Judgment: Whenever you *should* on someone, you are judging them. *He should be a better person. She should be home this time of the night. Why are they wearing those outfits? They should do better.* Judgment can also be internal; *I should be a better person.* Judgment limits you from being your expansive self. Don't *should* on yourself or others.

Kindness: Beholding benevolence toward yourself and others. Demonstrating a compassionate demeaner in the world.

Loneliness: Feeling alone, often when no one is around, but can also be felt when in the presence of others; you may feel disconnected when the relationship loses its meaning. You might also feel separate from people when they don't feel comfortable sharing themselves due to their social, cultural, or financial differences. Rule-followers and Givers who overextend themselves can feel they have no time for themselves, which can create a sense of loneliness from within.

Love: Creation of connection without judgment or resistance; the light force of spiritual awareness; collaboration; peace.

Melancholy: Felt when you experience a loss of hope. You sense the fire has gone out of your effort. You may think: *What's the use?*

Manipulation: The Oxford Dictionary states, "exercising unscrupulous control over a person or situation." In the presence of manipulators, you experience strong feelings of disconnection from your well-being, and your mental health suffers. The stress builds up and distorts your ability to perform productively. Resentment or fear can take over your thinking.

Nervousness: Typical emotion akin to worrying, anxiety, and fear. It appears most often regarding circumstances that are going to happen: you have to perform in some way, awaiting an event, or worrying about something that may or may not happen. Risk and uncertainty of the outcome are often associated with nervousness. It can be felt with positive or negative events and activities.

Overwhelm: Feeling your capacity has been surpassed by an overabundance of responsibilities and demands. Overwhelm creates an inability to sleep soundly and creates unhappy and depressed emotions. A sense of inner peace is unattainable, and problems seem too much to handle. It can also negatively affect your sense of worth. You can feel overwhelmed about many things, such as relationships in family, friendships, work, money, aging parents, and illness.

Power: Understanding of internal source that supports your ability to create and manifest good.

Powerlessness: Thoughts of being helpless, weak; without resources or support.

Pride: Good sense of yourself and your abilities. If your pride is contingent upon the things you possess, you can be on a slippery slope because, if the possessions go away, how will it affect your sense of self? If you acquire many things that create your sense of pride, you are putting the value on what is outside yourself. Pride is your love for yourself.

Resentment: Building awareness that you are being treated differently when expectations are different than what is asked of or recognized by the majority in a group. You may think to yourself: *My mistake is greater than the other person who looks like the boss.* Your brain (the amygdala) processes this as fear and secretes stress hormones, such as adrenaline. In that state, you may think you can't express your true outrage. If you do express your displeasure, you may be labeled *angry* or *obstructionist* when it is merely a reaction to your perception of the unfair treatment or situation. Some people respond with other emotions that can surface. Anger is generally the start, and resentment will follow, as well as shame, disappointment, disgust, and self-righteous indignation or contempt.

Sadness: Begins as a sense of loss of something dear to you, such as a loss of people in your life or a special physical thing, such as a valuable possession. Prolonged sadness can lead to tiredness and loss of interest in things you once enjoyed.

Shame: You hold close something about yourself, not wanting others to know for fear they will judge you as unacceptable. It can stem from something you have done, but it can also exist in your perception with no concrete support for it. It becomes a story you have told yourself about what others said years ago, and because you believed them, you carry the idea with you years later.

Stress: Amalgamation of anger, nervousness, and frustration that, if prolonged, creates havoc on your organs and nervous system. Our bodies were not built for chronic stress. The body secretes hormones to alert your brain to be on the lookout. Your muscles tense up and your heart rate increases.

Uneasiness: Apprehensive feeling demonstrating agitation or anxiety in specific situations when you deem something unpleasant is about to take place.

Vibrance: Feeling enthusiastic; demonstrating dynamic energy, sparkling personality traits; to be around a vibrant person is to feel uplifted while in their presence.

Vulnerability: Feeling the need for support while also being concerned about leaving yourself open to possibly being hurt; lacking confidence and a feeling of certainty. Some consider it a sign of weakness to be vulnerable, while it is actually a sharp edge used to be real with yourself and others you trust. If you share with someone who could not handle your truth and concern, you learn to walk away wiser and willing to open up with those who honor and love your exposure.

Weariness: Varying degrees of tiredness in situations that are likely repetitive and unfulfilling.

Worry: Concern over an imaginary or specific looming problem.

Worthiness: Knowing you are innately worthy simply because you were born. You were born with innate gifts to give yourself and as service to others. In worthiness, we love as openly as we know how. Give yourself grace when you fall short of that goal. As soon as you realize you are holding back on love, you start again by preparing your heart and mind to do better next time. People who understand their worth speak kindly to themselves. No amount of verbal berating can increase worthiness. It's your ego's attempt to keep you thinking less of yourself. Your deepest yearning is to be you; therefore, you do not model yourself after anyone else's notion (past or present) of who you should be. These are the ideals of feeling your worthiness.

Yearning: Living with an intense desire or longing within your purpose; exhibiting a strong urge to accomplish an aspiration.

Resources

Atlas of the Heart. Brené Brown. Random House Audio, 2021.

Becoming Supernatural. Joe Dispenza. Hay House, 2017.

Breaking the Habit of Being Yourself. Joe Dispenza. Hay House, 2012.

Burnout: The Secret to Unlocking the Stress Cycle. Amelia Nagoski and Emily Nagoski. Random House, 2019.

Change Your Brain, Change Your Life. Daniel G. Amen. Harmony Books, 2015.

Choose Wonder Over Worry. Amber Rae. St. Martin's Press, 2018.

A Course in Miracles, 3rd edition. Dr. Helen Schucman. Foundation for Inner Peace, 2007.

Cringeworthy: A Theory of Awkwardness. Melissa Dahl. Penguin Group, 2018.

The Four Agreements. Don Miguel Ruiz. Amber-Allen Publishing, 1997.

Inward Bound: Exploring The Geography of Your Emotions. Sam Keen. Bantam Books, 1992.

Mind to Matter. Dawson Church. Hay House, 2019.

The Myth of Normal. Gabor Maté. Penguin Group, 2022.

Pedagogy of the Oppression. Paulo Freire. Bloomsbury Publishing, 2000.

Permission to Feel. Marc Brackett. Celadon Books, 2019.

The Power of Your Subconscious Mind. Joseph Murphy. Way to Success, 2019.

Power vs Force. David R. Hawkins. Veritas Publishing, 2012.

The Seat of the Soul. Gary Zukav. Simon & Schuster, 2007.

Stress Less, Accomplish More. Emily Fletcher. Harper Collins Publisher, 2019.

Thinking 101. Woo-kyounh Ahn. Flatiron Books, 2022.

What Happened to You? Bruce Perry and Oprah Winfrey. Flatiron Books: An Oprah Book, 2021.

The Way of Integrity. Martha Beck. Penguin Group, 2021.

Connect With the Author

You can reach Deborah Liverett via the following media outlets:

Website
DeborahLiverett.com for inspirational content,
new release updates, and promotional offers

Instagram
@deborahliverett for her travel photography and inspiring messages

LinkedIn
Deborah Liverett Author

Facebook
Deborah Liverett

About the Author

Deborah Liverett is a survivor of several childhood and adult traumas which led her to read and study over one thousand books on healing, emotions, brain activity, and better living systems.

She used her inspirational coaching expertise as a manager for nearly thirty-two years of her thirty-eight years in Corporate America. Deborah recently retired from Northern Trust, an international financial company. She served as a Senior Vice President and Director of Community Affairs after twenty-five years of service and was an award-winning executive in corporate philanthropy. Deborah and her team helped to fund underserved global communities to support mothers and their children experiencing education, health, and housing difficulties around the globe.

Deborah is the founder of Live Life Coaching. Her first book, *Bread and Butter: A Self-Directed Discovery to Your Desired Life*, is available on Amazon. She recently contributed a chapter called "Still I Live" in an Amazon best-selling anthology, *Turning Point Moments, Volume 2*.

She graduated magna cum laude from North Carolina Central University, Coach Training Alliance, and has continually attended numerous growth and mindset trainings.